What People are Saying

"As a teacher of Julie's I am proud of her active and searching mind and how she brings what she has learned into the world. She has digested the teachings that matter most to her and she viscerally truth-checks her concepts in her body. She offers these teachings to other busy moms who are determined to grow in her book, *Vivid Living for Busy Moms*."

Ana Forrest
Creator of Forrest Yoga, and
Author of *Fierce Medicine*
www.forrestyoga.com

"A must read for moms! Powerful! Life Changing! In just seven 'sessions' Julie will warmly and expertly give you the coaching tools you need to tap into the innate wisdom of your mind and body to define and live what is absolutely most important to you in your life as a busy mom."

Kim George
Author of the best-seller
Coaching Into Greatness
and founder of *The Abundance Intelligence Institute*®
www.AbundanceIntelligence.com

"Working with Julie, I learned so much more about myself than I thought possible in a short amount of time. The exercises in this book made it much easier for me to bring my best self to every aspect of my life, from school and work, to my family and my marriage. And to top it all off, life coaching is fun! It didn't feel like work at all – more like I got to spend a lot of time with someone I've come to like a lot…ME!"

Lynne McIntyre
Documentary Film Maker, MSW,
and Mom of Two

Vivid Living
FOR BUSY MOMS

Vivid Living for Busy Moms.
Copyright © 2011 by Julie Zeff, MSW, CPCC.

All rights reserved. Printed and bound in the United States of America. No part of this book maybe used or reproduced by any means, graphic, electronic, or mechanical, including photocopying, recording, taping, or by any information storage retrieval system without the written permission of the author except in the case of brief quotations embodied in critical articles and reviews.

ISBN-13: 978-1461138600

ISBN-10: 1461138604

Library of Congress Control Number: 2011910432

The author assumes no responsibility for errors, omissions, or inconsistencies herein. Every effort has been made to ensure the material presented is accurate, that the information presented is current and up to date and that Internet addresses were active at the time of printing. The information and recommendations in this book are presented in good faith and for general information purposes only. This book should not be considered a substitute for advice from medical, mental health, financial, or legal professionals. The advice and strategies contained herein may not be suitable for your situation. You should consult with a professional where appropriate. The author and any affiliated companies shall have neither liability nor responsibility to any person or entity with respect to any loss or damage caused or alleged to have been caused, directly or indirectly, by the information contained in this book.

The names used in some of the personal stories in this book have been changed at the participants' request.

Cover and layout designed by Anna Rubio, www.conceptostudio.com
and Deborah Perdue of Illumination Graphics. www.illuminationgraphics.com

Back Cover Photo by Rutti Simon. www.imagineitonline.com

Attention Corporations, Universities, Colleges and Professional Organizations: Quantity discounts are available on bulk purchases of this book for educational, gift purposes, or as premiums for increasing magazine subscriptions or renewals. Special books or book excerpts can also be created to fit specific needs. For information, please contact Julie Zeff, Julie@vividliving.net. www.vividliving.net

Vivid Living
FOR BUSY MOMS

Coach Yourself to an Extraordinary Life

Julie Zeff, MSW, CPCC

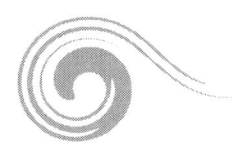

Dedication

To the love of my life, my best friend, and my live-in life coach, Ken Zeff.

Table of Contents

INTRODUCTION 13

    The Beginning of Vivid Living...Julie's Story 13

    How To Get The Most From This Book 19

    Create A Vivid Living Group or Buddy Up! 25

SESSION I 31
You've Got Yourself a Life Coach

SESSION II 45
Take Your Life's Temperature

SESSION III 73
Listen to Your BodyTruth

SESSION IV 109
Get to Your Core

SESSION V 145
Your Life Purpose

SESSION VI 169
Get Those Ogres

SESSION VII 197
Build Your Toolbox

ABOUT THE AUTHOR 220

Acknowledgements

A HUGE thank you to my courageous clients, on the phone and on the yoga mat, who have shown me the way to vivid and extraordinary living. Your unyielding quest to live your truth and a life you love inspires me daily! Your continued belief in our work together gave me the confidence and impetus to share this life-changing work with the world.

A special thank you to all of you moms (and some non-moms out there) who lent your inspiring stories to this book. It wouldn't have the depth and richness it does without your bold and courageous sharing.

To my Vivid Living "Board of Directors" who over the past two years has supported me and tolerated the million and one emails and phone calls asking for feedback and suggestions, to read chapters or even the whole book, or to run pilot Vivid Living Groups with friends or colleagues. Your tireless encouragement and inspiration kept me moving forward at times when I felt stuck and the light seemed dim. Thank you to Laurie Saroff, Alison Welch, Eva Gordon, Marc Fienberg, Beth Stiner, Lynne McIntyre, Sagit Piken, Jodi Marion, Barb Mudrick, Aaron Stiner, and Jennifer Pellman.

Thank you to all of my fellow authors and coaches, Gail Barrie, Kate Hanley, Marlena Field, Alexia Brue, Hallie Crawford, and Kim George. You inspired me to honor my own "book-writing" spark. You paved the way and showed me that I could do it, too. Thank you to Therese Kienast, my very first life coach, who passionately ushered me into the world of coaching and introduced me to the concept of Essences.

Thank you to Ana Forrest. Your yoga changed my life. I breathe in life more deeply, live from my heart more fully, and walk taller, stronger, and braver because of you.

Thank you to my two editors, Alison Welch and Dan Zeff, for catching my mistakes and helping me to share my message and passion clearly with the world! Thank you to my two cover and layout designers, Anna Rubio and Deborah Perdue. Anna, you took the vivid yet sacred essence of this work and began the creation process. Deborah, you picked up this precious project, saw right to the heart of it and me and breathed color and life into it. Thank you to Rutti Simon for your inspiring photography.

Thank you to my live-in life coach and adoring husband, Ken Zeff, for believing in and seeing the absolute best in me, always! Thank you for putting up with all of those frozen dinners and "Hi" grunts when I was on the computer writing when you got home from work. And, for knowing how deeply important this book is to me. I love you like crazy!!

Thank you to my three amazing kids, Audrey, Sarah, and Jonah Zeff. Your smiles, laughter, and curiosity make my heart swell with overflowing joy. You have ushered me into motherhood. It has not always been a graceful journey, but it has been a beautiful and deeply gratifying one. The three of you have given my life more purpose and meaning than I ever imagined possible. You are my sacred teachers! "Team Zeff" is the most precious gift of my life.

Thank you to my parents, Allen Schwartz and Sharon Maurer-Schwartz, and my "other mother," Ande Rice. You always encouraged me to follow my dreams and passions. And, you taught me how to love.

INTRODUCTION

The Beginning of Vivid Living… Julie's Story

My Vivid Living journey began in 1995 when I discovered the transformative power of combining the wisdom of the mind and the body. My path unfolded (and is still unfolding) step by teeny, tiny step. When I wasn't sure which way to turn, I kept following my heart and passion. I have now gloriously found my way here – to today – to *Vivid Living for Busy Moms*!

Let me take you back a couple of years. My mother was a psychotherapist in private practice, so I grew up with psychotherapists all around me. In 1995, I had a life-changing experience when I started working as a client with a mind/body psychotherapist. This psychotherapist combined touch with psychotherapy – a new concept for me at the time. She laid her hand on my back in places where she identified tightness or holding. I then breathed into those places and noticed what memories, images, colors, or sensations appeared.

By sharing what I noticed with her, I gained access to breakthroughs unlike any I had previously experienced. The work was absolutely transformational for me. I began to let go of old patterns and beliefs that no longer served me and started to access my strength and truth in new ways. From that point on I was hooked. I absolutely believed in the profound transformative power of combining the wisdom of the mind and the body.

Around that same time, I graduated from college with a degree in English/Creative Writing and obtained a teaching certificate. With noble intentions I gave inner-city English teaching a try. Although I love literature, I found I had very little interest in teaching *The Scarlet Letter* to high school students. I was much more interested in understanding their family dynamics.

This curiosity led me to enroll in a graduate program for social work. Following in the footsteps of my amazing mind/body therapist, I decided that I, too, wanted to combine bodywork and psychotherapy. I enrolled in massage therapy school while in graduate school.

In 1997, I graduated from the Chicago School of Massage Therapy and in 1998 I completed my master's degree in social work from the University of Chicago. I began working at a social service agency in a Chicago suburb doing individual, couple, family, and group psychotherapy. Over the next three years, I persistently and unsuccessfully tried to figure out how to combine bodywork and psychotherapy.

Over time I felt discouraged, uncertain, and lost. I left my job as a social worker and explored what I wanted to be when I grew up. I traveled solo in Europe for six weeks (which had been a lifelong dream of mine) and took myself through the book *What Color is Your Parachute* by Richard Bolles.

I held informational interviews with people in different fields – people in business, health care, and psychology. I met amazing people, learned about life coaching for the first time, and interviewed a few life coaches myself. They were some of the happiest, warmest, dynamic, and exciting people I had ever met. Their energy was contagious and I remember thinking that I wanted whatever drug they were taking. The drug, as it turns out, was life coaching.

At that time I wasn't quite ready to take the plunge into the field of life coaching. With persistence and some luck in 2002, I found a job in Human Resources and Organizational Development with a large global bank in Chicago. I quickly realized that although I enjoyed the fast-paced, dynamic life of working for a large organization, ultimately it wasn't for me.

Around this time I became engaged to my best friend and now my husband, Ken Zeff. The momentous life change in front of me brought me to hire my own life coach. After working with my own coach for three weeks, I was ready. I realized that I absolutely wanted to be a life coach, too. I loved the practical, empowering, and strengths-based approach to the work.

From the beginning, life coaching focused on everything I was doing right. It built on my strengths, passions, and encouraged me to keep tapping into my truth that I found by listening to my mind and body. Here it was again: that glorious mind/body connection.

It was just what I needed to gain a new level of trust in myself and my decision-making abilities. I got to know and trust myself like never before. And, around this same time, I introduced myself to yoga and loved it.

In 2002-2003, I completed the Basic and Advanced Coaching Training with CTI (Coaches Training Institute), married my husband, and began searching for a yoga teacher training program I felt would blend well with my newly budding coaching practice.

After exploring many different styles of yoga, I found what I was looking for – Forrest Yoga (developed by Ana Forrest). I was drawn to it instantly! Ana's work utilized many of the same concepts and ideas I implemented in my work with clients as a life coach. It emphasized breath awareness, being present in our bodies, and the notion that we are all powerful beings who are at choice in our mind, body, and life in every single moment. It was a natural fit.

Over the next five years, our expanding family moved around a lot. My husband's career in inner city school reform took us from Chicago to San Diego, to Washington, D.C., and back to the West Coast where we now live in Los Angeles. We had a child born in each city, and my coaching practice kept growing and growing amidst moves and maternity leave.

The individual and group coaching that I do is mostly over the phone. I've had clients in cities across the U.S. and in Europe who stayed with me from move to move and child to child. I've watched clients make courageous and life-altering changes as a result of our work together. I've seen them tap into their own wisdom and courage like never before. Empowered clients changed their lives and lived their dreams by harnessing just a few powerful coaching tools and focusing on their strength and passion.

Through coaching, my clients have:
- Learned to tap into the unique wisdom and language of their bodies and minds.

- Built trust in themselves to make decisions with confidence and clarity.

- Uncovered their true Life Purpose and Essences – who they are at their core.

- Lived in extraordinary ways they once thought impossible.

Here are just a few examples of client successes as a result of experiencing life coaching with me.
- Shari left the stability of a high-paying job and a city she once loved to live more passionately and create work-life balance.

- Sheryl found her soul mate and married him.

- Liz realized that she did, indeed, want to have another child.

- Jeffrey left a secure work situation and started his own company.

- Laurie decided to have another baby and go back to work full-time with confidence and guilt-free ease.

- Lisa put clear limits on her work and family time. She learned how to prioritize from her core and to say "No!" to her Blackberry, work expectations, and family obligations that weighed her down.

- Erica repaired damaged relationships with parents and siblings.

- Pam let go of stale friendships and created ones that energized her.

- Andre found the courage to move halfway around the globe to honor his dream of living abroad and starting his own company.

- Molly negotiated more me-time into her week – time away from her kids, family and work – and finally felt that guilt-free balance she had been craving.

These clients found their truth and answers not from me, their coach, but from looking within – getting curious and learning to trust the natural wisdom of their bodies and minds. They learned how to listen and summoned their own strength and courage to make the changes they knew would lead them to Vivid Living. They learned to be their own life coach.

In January 2009, our third child was born and so was the idea for this book. While on maternity leave I identified a yearning within to share the power of this work with as many people as possible. I realized how especially powerful and important this work is for busy and working moms.

Being a busy mom myself, I had been attracting other moms to my practice for years. They all had things in common. They were looking for more balance, less guilt, more space (me-time), increased peace, and to feel less alone and imperfect. They wanted to find that place of deep trust in themselves – to know exactly who they are now and what is most important in the midst of endless and competing responsibilities and priorities.

Suddenly, it became even more vital for me to share this work. There are so many moms out there today who crave more support, structures, and concrete tools to help them live a vivid life they love…not just one they like.

I created this book to make accessible to you the same tips and tools I use with my clients (and that I use myself). The tips and tools here will help you to tap into the unique wisdom and power of your body and mind – your truth and power – and will allow you to live a balanced, vivid, and extraordinary life you will love. I know because I have seen it work for my clients over the years. And, I know because it works for me every day.

Welcome to your Vivid Living journey!

Much Peace and Love,

Julie Zeff

Julie Zeff

How to Get the Most from This Book

Welcome, amazing mom! Here are a few suggestions to help you get the most you can from this book and the deeply rich experience you are about to dive into.

- **Go through this book solo, with a mom-buddy, or with a Vivid Living Group.** This is an exciting and dynamic journey. If you are a highly motivated individual, are good at holding yourself accountable, and like to work individually, then going through this book solo might be just right for you. If you are open to learning from the experience and wisdom of others and desire outside inspiration, support, and accountability to maintain lasting change in your life, then creating a Vivid Living Group or "buddying" up with another mom may be a great option for you. If you are interested in forming or facilitating a group or finding a buddy to go through this book with then read *Create a Vivid Living Group or Buddy Up* on page 25.

- **Make a date with yourself.** Commit to making time for this work, even though it may be challenging as a working mom. You can do it! Each session is full of new concepts, ideas, tools, and Journal and Action Exercises. Whether you meet with a group or go through this adventure alone, I encourage you to set a consistent meeting time to introduce yourself to each new session. If you are doing this solo, I suggest you commit to **one hour every week/month** to read through the new session and to begin the Journal or Action Exercises. Make a date with yourself to do it.

    For everyone, I suggest committing to **15 minutes a day** to do the exercises, write/journal, or consciously practice and think about this new material. This time is really important because it will help to bring the Journal and Action Exercises alive and consciously put in place your new habits and patterns.

The more time and attention you give this work (really, that you give **yourself**), the bigger the payoff. Some moms wake up before everyone else in their house just to have 15 minutes all to themselves. Some take 15 minutes to think about this work or to journal before going to bed. Some do it over lunch – a lunch date with themselves. Some take a break in the afternoon or mid-morning. See what works for you. Say "Yes!" to yourself. You absolutely **do** (even if you think you don't) have 15 minutes a day to transform your life!

- **Write and make this book your own**. Write in this book, draw pictures, use colors, fold down pages, and add in any inspiring items you collect along the way. The more interactive you make this experience the more you'll get out of it. There is space after each exercise for you to capture your thoughts and experiences. If you don't have enough room in the space provided feel free to use the additional blank page at the end of each session, clip in your own pages, or buy a special journal dedicated to Vivid Living and capturing your adventures and explorations.

- **You don't need to do all of the Journal or Action Exercises in this book!** You'll get all the tools YOU need to live a vivid life you love if you read through the Journal and Action Exercises and do the ones that stand out, inspire, excite or challenge you the most. If journaling is new to you or isn't your thing, then know that your journaling doesn't have to be perfect, long, or profound. Simply capture whatever you notice or whatever is on your mind. Getting down a few words, sentences, pictures, or even scribbles can help you to tap into your own wisdom, truth, and experience in a new way. Try it!

- **Give yourself homework.** In order to make the most of this experience, I suggest that you commit to at least one homework assignment at the end of every session. Together, my clients and I find one to five energizing homework assignments for them after every call. These are things for you to practice, journal about, or experiment with before you dive into the next session. Homework will help you get where you want to go and deepen your connection with what you are learning. Use the What's My Homework? page at the end of sessions II-VII to write down your homework and commitments.

- **Be willing to experiment and to fail.** Many of these ideas and concepts may be new to you. Permit yourself to try them out fully, mess up, fall on your face, and be perfectly imperfect. By experimenting with these new ways of being, stretching outside of your comfort zone, and moving beyond what is familiar, you'll make the changes necessary to live a vivid and extraordinary life you'll love. If what you were doing before wasn't getting you a life you love then try something different. Dream and think big.

- **Visualization suggestions.** You'll have many opportunities to practice doing visualizations throughout this book. Visualizations are great for getting your mind and body to work together. There is no one right or wrong way to do visualizations. Here is a process you can follow to get the most out of the visualizations if doing them is new to you.

    1. **Find a quiet space.** Feel free to sit, lie down, or be in any comfortable position in which you can easily relax.

    2. **Read the questions.** Read through one set of questions at a time. Then close your eyes.

    3. **Breathe.** Take a few relaxing, deep breaths and ask yourself the questions you just read.

4. **Notice.** Notice whatever you experience in your mind and body. Know that there is no "right" or "wrong" answer. Be with whatever comes and use my words as a guide. Trust your own experience. As you get into the visualization you might hear words, see images and colors, recall memories, smell smells, feel feelings, or experience sensations in your body. Anything and everything is welcome!

5. **Capture it.** Be with whatever you notice for a few breaths. Be open and curious. Then take some time to capture, in writing or pictures, whatever it is that you noticed. Use the space provided in this book or attach additional sheets of paper.

    If you aren't a big fan of visualizations, you can still take yourself through the steps and questions. Just keep your eyes open.

- **Notice the Ogres**. The biggest roadblocks to Vivid Living are usually your internal ones – the naysayers and the voices of fear, doubt and sabotage that hold you back and keep you from your greatness. I choose to call these voices Ogres. If you have a different name for this part of yourself, use it. I'll give you some tips for how to deal with these sneaky suckers in session VI, "Get Those Ogres." Meanwhile, don't be surprised if your Ogres pop up or get louder as you make your way through this book. They are committed to keeping things just the way they are and to making you miserable. As you start thinking about and creating a vivid and extraordinary life you love and your Ogres pop up, just wave at them. Then move right past them. Just because they are loud or obtrusive doesn't mean they are TRUE. **You can still move forward even with fears and doubts**.

- **Brave and Bold Questions**

  > Sprinkled throughout this book you'll find Brave and Bold Questions in boxes like this one. They are represented by this symbol. 🆎 These questions are here to help you dig deeper. Don't let them slip by without at least thinking about your response. Better yet, write your answers in the margins or in your Vivid Living journal. Let your curiosity and adventurous spirit run wild.

- **Digital Downloads**

  Anytime you see this symbol ⬇ you know that a fun or helpful Digital Download is available from my website. To download it, simply visit www.vividliving.net/freebookdownloads. Get an extra juicy bit of Vivid Living!

- **Create Structures**

  A structure is a reminder – something to bring you back to your enlivening exploration or homework between sessions. It's easy to get excited about your commitments and intentions. The hard part is keeping them. In order to make the changes you intend, it is essential that these new ideas stay front and center. Here are just a few suggestions for structures you can use. Feel free to develop your own – be creative. I encourage you to revisit this list often as you go through the following sessions.

  > ⬇
  > Structures will help you keep this work front and center. Visit www.vividliving.net/freebookdownloads to download this **Suggested Structures List**. Post it up and keep it close.

Suggested Structures List

- **Write it.** Write down your commitments/homework on the What's My Homework? page provided at the end of sessions II-VII.

- **Tell someone.** When we share our commitments out loud it often makes them more real.

- **Ask for accountability.** Ask someone to check in with you and hold you accountable to your commitments.

- **Calendar it.** Put your commitments into your calendar or datebook each day. Make a date with yourself to do them.

- **Create sticky notes.** Make sticky notes and decorate your home, car, or office with them.

- **Put up pictures.** Find a screen saver/pictures with an inspiring image or words that represent what you are trying to create or want for yourself so you see it often.

- **Wear jewelry.** Wear a new or different piece of jewelry, or wear old jewelry in a different way (different wrist or finger) to remind you of what you want to remember.

- **Set an alarm.** Set an alarm every day, or every hour, to remind you of your commitment.

- **Pick an object.** Find an item like a rock, picture, song, poem, or stuffed animal that reminds you of your commitment. Put it in a prominent place or even in your pocket, purse, or wallet.

- **Use daily living reminders.** Use things in your busy everyday mom-world to serve as structures. Commit to thinking about a new idea, tool or something you want to remember when you stop at red lights, do the dishes, while you are in the shower, packing lunches, or walking the dog.

Create a Vivid Living Group or Buddy Up

Does going through this book with a mom-buddy or group of other moms sound exciting or intriguing to you? Do you get inspired by hearing other's stories? Are you more likely to make changes in your life if you are held accountable for your actions? Do you like book groups or meeting with others to share your thoughts? If so, then I strongly encourage you to form your own Vivid Living Group or find yourself a mom-buddy. (I use the term "group" below, but please feel free to insert the word "buddy" if you are going to share this experience with just one other person.)

This work is exciting, powerful, deep, and life-changing. Sharing it with other busy moms can give it even more depth and staying power in your life. Time and time again I hear from moms who participated in Vivid Living Groups about how invaluable participating in a group was for them. So much of their learning and inspiration for change came directly from sharing with other moms in the group. They had built-in accountability, a place to ask questions, and a source of feedback, support, and encouragement along the way. Most of all they learned they are not alone!

Here are tips for creating your own Vivid Living Group. Please feel free to be creative and find what works for you, your group, or buddy.

1. **Who could be in my group?** Look to your circle of friends, family, colleagues, and acquaintances to find other moms you think may be interested in joining you on a Vivid Living Group adventure. If you are already part of a book club, mom or parents' group, support group, or professional group, that could be a great place to start.

   All of the coaching I do is over the phone, so feel free to create a group with people in different geographic locations – there are many free teleconference options out there. (See the Vivid Living Resources page at the end of this session for more information about the free conference line I use.) Telecalls can be a great option for busy moms!

2. **How many people could I have in a group?** I suggest forming a group with between 3-10 people in it.

3. **How often do we meet?** Decide on a regular time to meet in person or over the phone. The regularity would depend on your availability and how much time you want to explore the learning in between sessions.

4. **Confidentiality.** This one is a biggie! Agree to keep all that occurs in your group confidential so you create a safe space in which to be daring and courageous.

5. **How long is a meeting?** Allow at least 60-minutes for each meeting if you have a buddy and 90-minutes if you are part of a group.

6. **Who leads the group?** The same person can facilitate every meeting or you can rotate. It is the facilitator's job to watch the time for the meeting and to keep people focused and moving forward.

7. **How do we structure each group?** I suggest a half and half approach. Focus the first half of each meeting on reviewing successes, challenges, and questions. This discussion time is a precious time to share, encourage, and challenge yourself and each other. The second half can be spent on the new material. It can be helpful to read the new material aloud. Then talk about any questions that come up and choose one or two Journal or Action Exercises to complete and discuss together as a group.

8. **Suggestions for the first group meeting.** Spend the first half of the group time getting to know each other. Below are some

suggestions. The second half of the group time can be spent going over the new material.

    a. Have each person share her name.

    b. Have each person share what she hopes to get out of the group.

    c. The facilitator can choose one or two icebreakers from the list below.

- Share one thing that is unique about you or that most people don't know about you.
- Share one fun thing that you like to do.
- Share something that you are really good at.
- Share a sweet memory from when you were little.

9. **Ending a group.** Before ending each group I suggest the facilitator give each person one minute to share any of the following:

- What stood out most for them from the session.
- What they learned.
- What they are curious about.
- What they are committing to for homework.
- How they want the group to support them or help to hold them accountable.

Or, have everyone spend the last minute or two writing down their commitments and homework.

10. **Communicate and share between meetings.** Set up a way to email or connect between groups so you can share learnings,

challenges, or questions. You can share phone numbers and email addresses, or set up a discussion group online – like a Yahoo! Group.

11. **Have fun, get curious, be creative, and go live a vivid and extraordinary life you love!**

Visit www.vividliving.net/freebookdownloads to download and print out this section if you wish to have it in your hands during a Vivid Living Group or Buddy Up session.

Vivid Living Resources

INTRODUCTION

FREE Digital Downloads

⊕ **Suggested Structures List.** Download and/or print a copy of this list. It will remind you of just a few possible structures to help keep this work alive.

www.vividliving.net/freebookdownloads

⊕ **Create a Vivid Living Group or Buddy Up!** Download and print out this section if you wish to have it in your hands during a Vivid Living Group or Buddy Up session.

www.vividliving.net/freebookdownloads

Vivid Living Blog
Check it out!
www.vividliving.net/blog

Read my posts and connect with others who are on the path to Vivid Living. Get (maybe even give) some inspiration. We're all in this together!

Additional Resource

Totally Free Conference Calls. I have used this resource for all of my group calls for the past four years and really like them.
www.totallyfreeconferencecalls.com

Notes

You've Got Yourself a Life Coach

SESSION 1

Twenty years from now you will be more disappointed by the things that you didn't do than by the ones you did do. So throw off the bowlines. Sail away from the safe harbor. Catch the trade winds in your sails.
Explore. Dream. Discover.
Mark Twain

Change is inevitable. Growth is optional.
Anonymous

Welcome, busy mom! Congratulations on making it here. I know your life is busy and full of more responsibilities than you know how to manage some days. Maybe you work, take care of your children, your home, sometimes even your partner, and the family schedule. Maybe you give to your community, your friends, and your extended family, too. Keeping it all together can be exhausting and challenging. Finding a moment all to yourself is a huge feat. So, congratulate yourself for simply reading this paragraph right now. If you are, it means you created a precious moment of space for yourself! That is definitely something to celebrate!

I, too, am a busy mom. I work, have three children under the age of seven, and am very involved in my children's schools and our community. All of what I do feeds me. I am a better, more fulfilled, and all around happier mom and person because of all that I do. But, it definitely is a juggling act. Sometimes it feels like there are way more balls in the air than I can keep afloat with just my two hands.

Over the years, working as a life coach and yoga instructor, I've coached many busy moms. I have collected an array of powerful tools that help me and my clients to stay focused on what is most important, enjoyable, and fulfilling in any given moment. I have the tools that will help you to become crystal clear about who you are at your core, tap into your absolute truth, and live a vivid and extraordinary life you love!

I am going to take you on a journey much like the one through which I lead my clients. All of the major life coaching concepts, tips, and tools I share with my clients are embedded in the sessions in this book.

Join me, session by session, to learn new tools to engage your body and mind (you need both working together), so you can ultimately create and live a vivid and extraordinary life you love. Experience first-hand, the amazing and transformative power of life coaching. Let's jump in…

Vivid Living!

We all want one – a vivid and extraordinary life we love. But, how do you get one and what the heck is Vivid Living anyway? Everyone's definition of Vivid Living will be different.

I will tell you one thing – Vivid Living is not perfect living or having a perfect life. After working for over 10 years as a Life Coach and in the mental health field, I can say with certainty that no one has a perfect life. It just doesn't exist. So, you can stop trying to create one for yourself right now.

Vivid Living is living a life YOU love. Not a life your friends, spouse, parents, children or colleagues would love, but a vivid life YOU love.

By the time you are finished with this book, you'll know what Vivid Living looks and feels like for YOU, and you'll have the tools you need to create and live it.

You'll know exactly where your life is out of balance and what you can do to balance it. You'll know how to tap into the innate language and wisdom of your body. You'll understand who you really are at your core, and discover the things that make you the real YOU. You'll identify what is most important to you and your Life Purpose. You'll recognize how you limit yourself so you can leap over sabotaging land mines or free yourself up if you happen to get tangled. You'll have the tools to wake up excited every morning. You'll know and trust yourself like never before.

And, If I have done my job well, I will have coached myself out of job. You will, in essence, be your own life coach, living a vivid life YOU love.

The Vivid Living Journey

Here are the themes for your upcoming coaching sessions.

Session I – You've Got Yourself a Life Coach

Session II – Take Your Life's Temperature

Session III – Listen to Your BodyTruth

Session IV – Get to Your Core

Session V – Live Your Life Purpose

Session VI – Get Those Ogres

Session VII – Build Your Tool Box

Here is the general structure of each session.

- I begin each session by introducing a new concept. I'll define and describe it and then I'll share some of my own personal examples and client examples to help illuminate the way, clarify questions, and inspire you.

- Each session ends with Session Highlights that summarize the main points from the session.

- After the Highlights section in sessions II-VII, you'll find specific Journal Exercises to help you deepen your learning and Action Exercises to help you intentionally leap forward. These exercises serve as your homework - things for you to practice or explore between sessions. I've included lots of them for you in the hopes that a few of them will resonate. **You do NOT need to do them all**.

Simply pick out a couple of Journal or Action Exercises for each session that speak to you. Look for the ones that challenge or excite you. Do the ones you think will help you get closer to what you want more of for yourself. Trust that you'll do just the right ones.

- You can write down the homework you commit to exploring on the What's My Homework? page following the Journal and Action Exercises in sessions II-VII. Writing down your commitments will help you to follow through.

- Check out the Vivid Living Resources page near the end of each session to find fun, helpful, and inspiring downloads and other resources to keep you moving forward.

- At the end of sessions II-VII you'll have a chance to do a Vivid Living Check-In before heading on to the next session. Here you get to capture your learning, challenges, and any specific tips or tools you want to remember as you soar forward on your Vivid Living adventure. You'll also get a chance to take your life's temperature using the Vivid Living Thermometer. Use this tool to track how your life is changing from one session to the next.

Every session in this book will build on the next just as it does with my clients. There is no magic formula or one-size-fits-all-approach to learn the tools for Vivid Living. I've put the sessions in this book in an order that I think will give you the best access to these new concepts. When I work with clients, however, I vary the order and most often weave these concepts in and out of the work depending on what each client desires and brings to each session.

I suggest that you first follow along in the order presented here and get familiar with all the tools. Then feel free to weave the tips and tools together in any way that works for you. How and when to use these tools will be become clearer as you make your way through this book.

Explore, play, and challenge your edges. Allow yourself the space and time to think about the new ideas you'll uncover in each session. Embrace what excites and enlivens you. Use these tools. Practice them. Make them a part of your daily life. If you do, you'll be living a vivid life you love in no time.

If you're ready (or even if you're on the fence or a bit nervous) let's dive in. Vivid and extraordinary living is waiting!

Vivid Living JumpStart Survey

For your first homework assignment, I invite you to complete the JumpStart Survey that I send to all clients before we begin our work together. This survey gives you a baseline to begin working from and will help you to get your coaching juices flowing.

Most clients come to me looking for guidance, clarity, and deeper and more powerful ways to get to know and trust themselves. Simply filling out the JumpStart Survey is a fabulous first step. It can give you insight into who you are, what you most desire, and what gets in your way.

Fill it out. Get a sense of the general flavor of your writing and answers. Do you feel hopeful, depressed, excited, detailed, hesitant, etc., as you write? Notice what stands out for you.

If it feels like you don't know the answer to a question, don't worry. Just do the best you can. Fill in something anyway, even if you aren't sure about it. See what comes. Whatever it is will be just right. Be as thorough and honest as you can in answering these questions. The more open you are, the more you'll get out of this process.

At the end of the JumpStart Survey, you'll have a chance to fill in your Main Aim and spell out what you intend to focus on or transform as you move through your Vivid Living journey. If you're not exactly sure of what to write here, that's OK. Just put down the first things that pop into your head or anything you think you'd like to change or shift in your life.

Some changes you plan to make will be obvious, easy, fun, and will feel really good. Other transformations will be harder and might frustrate, challenge, and maybe even terrify you. If it was easy to change you probably would have done it already and you certainly wouldn't need this book.

So, muster up all the strength and courage you have within and take the big leap. This is your time and your one and only life. Why not make it fabulous? Trust and know that you absolutely have what it takes to live a vivid and extraordinary life you love.

After you complete the JumpStart Survey, I'll meet you for your next coaching session. Welcome!

Vivid Living JumpStart Survey

> If you wish to fill out the JumpStart Survey on a separate sheet of paper go to www.vividliving.net/freebookdownloads to download a copy of the **Vivid Living JumpStart Survey**. Feel free to share it and to use it to spark conversation with your spouse, friends, family, or colleagues.

Date: _____

1. What events or accomplishments must occur in your lifetime for you to feel satisfied and have few, if any, regrets?

2. Assuming your lifestyle was the same as it is today but your income was unlimited, what would you love to do?

3. What is missing from your life that would make it more fulfilling?

4. What are you passionate about? What gets your blood pumping?

5. What roles do you see yourself having personally, professionally, and in the community?

6. What behaviors or habits do you fight? What blind spots or hot buttons keep you from success?

7. What challenges continually confront you?

8. **Your Main Aim**

    Identify three to five goals or intentions you want to hold as your Main Aim during this coaching process. What do you want more of in your life? What do you want to transform? Write it all down here and get as specific as possible.

    Rate yourself on a scale of 0 to 10 on how much you have achieved your Main Aim as of today. You'll get to score yourself again at the end of this book to see how far you've come and what has changed.

MAIN AIM	SCORE 0-10 10=Most & 0=Least
Example: My life feels balanced. I feel balanced.	3
1.	
2.	
3.	
4.	
5.	

Vivid Living Resources

SESSION I

FREE Digital Downloads

⬇ **Vivid Living JumpStart Survey.** Download as many copies as you wish of the JumpStart Survey here. Share it!

www.vividliving.net/freebookdownloads

Recommended Reading
Co-Active Coaching: New Skills For Coaching People Toward Success by Laura Whitworth, Karen Kimsey-House, Henry Kimsey-House, Phillip Sandahl.

Notes

Notes

Take Your Life's Temperature

SESSION II

> *When you walk to the edge of all the light you have and take the first step into the darkness of the unknown, you must believe that one of two things will happen: There will be something solid for you to stand upon, or, you will be taught how to fly.*
> **Patrick Overton**

> *To be surprised, to wonder, is to begin to understand.*
> **Jose Ortega y Gasset**

So, you've completed your JumpStart Survey or at least looked it over and are ready for more.

Fabulous!

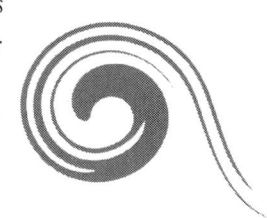

As a busy mom, I bet you have lots of responsibilities on your plate and many obligations competing for your attention. You know your life is full, maybe even overflowing, but do you know exactly what areas of your life are out of balance or what parts could use *some extra attention? In this session I'll introduce you to a tool to help you get a sense of what's "hot" and what's "not" in your life.*

So, let's get curious and take your life's temperature!

The Vivid Living Thermometer

The Vivid Living Thermometer is a tool made up of the 11 most important areas of your life: Career, Environment, Family, Friends, Fun, Health, Me as Mom, Money, Personal Growth, Significant Other, and Spirituality.

It is a great place to begin to assess how much you are (or are not) living a vivid and extraordinary life you love. It is the first tool I use with each and every client. Clients love it because it is a quantifiable way to track growth and progress over time.

It is simple and accessible. It can help you get clear about the areas you want to transform and the areas you want to celebrate as you embark on your Vivid Living coaching adventure.

If you aren't quite sure where to start to get yourself living a vivid and extraordinary life you love, then the Vivid Living Thermometer will help. It will bring your attention to the areas of your life that want some tender loving care and will help you to identify your next steps for improving those areas.

I often suggest to clients that we begin every coaching session by filling in a Vivid Living Thermometer. This focuses them in the moment and gives them a chance to acknowledge the progress they've made from week to week.

Your Turn!

Now it's your turn to fill in your very own Vivid Living Thermometer. Follow the instructions below to fill in the blank Vivid Living Thermometer on page 48. *If you want to see an example, then look at my (Julie's) personal Vivid Living Thermometer on page 51.*

1. **Date it**. Put today's date on the top of the page/list.

2. **Breathe**. Take a few breaths.

3. **Rate it.** Give each area of your life a rating between 0-10. Zero is the worst it could ever be, 10 is the best it could ever be. Write the rating/number in the space provided next to each area. Go with the first number that pops into your head. Don't over think it. There is no right or wrong here. More than one area can have the same rating. At the end, give yourself a final Overall Vivid Living rating too.

4. **Notice**. What stands out most for you after filling in your Vivid Living Thermometer? Compare your ratings today to those of your previous Vivid Living Thermometers (if applicable). Celebrate the "hot" areas. Then notice which areas of your life could use some more attention.

5. **Commit and transform.** Which areas do you want to shift? Write the area/s you plan to give some extra attention to on the Area of Focus line. Next, write the commitment/s you are making that will raise the rating of that area on the Commitment line. *If you aren't sure what to write here, no worries! Going through the rest of this session and the Journal and Action Exercises will give you some ideas.*

Visit www.vividliving.net/freebookdownloads to download a blank copy of the **Vivid Living Thermometer**. Feel free to share it!

VIVID LIVING THERMOMETER   Date _____

AREA OF YOUR LIFE	RATING 0-10
CAREER	
ENVIRONMENT	
FAMILY	
FRIENDS	
FUN	
HEALTH	
ME AS MOM	
MONEY	
PERSONAL GROWTH	
SIGNIFICANT OTHER	
SPIRITUALITY	
OVERALL VIVID LIVING	

AREA OF FOCUS _____
COMMITMENT _____
_____

> What would having all 10's on your Vivid Living Thermometer look and feel like in your day-to-day life? Close your eyes and let yourself feel and imagine it for a few moments

Sarah's Story

Sarah came to her first individual coaching session dissatisfied with her life and ready to make some changes. She was an overwhelmed working mom of three who hadn't taken time for herself in over two years. She worked over 50 hours a week at her job and put every one else's needs before her own. She was tired!

We began with a Vivid Living Thermometer check-in and her numbers were low. She felt stuck and even a bit hopeless about making the changes she wanted to make in her life. By the time we completed our coaching work together her numbers were high and her feelings and perspective about her life had shifted dramatically. It was easy to see this shift, in part, because we used the Vivid Living Thermometer at the beginning of every session together to track her progress along the way.

You, too, will have an opportunity to regularly revisit the Vivid Living Thermometer before you begin each new session. You'll be able to see and track the changes you are making as you move through this book.

> How could regularly using the Vivid Living Thermometer help you to live a vivid and extraordinary life you love?

Perspective not Perfection

Clients often ask me if it is possible to have all 10's on the Vivid Living Thermometer. The answer is yes. Clients also ask me if you have to have all 10's on the Vivid Living Thermometer to be living a truly vivid and extraordinary life. The answer is no.

So, how could these both be true? The answer lies in your perspective and the power of choice. Here are some examples.

I remember one week in particular when I was writing this book. I devoted much of my work time (and free time) to it that week. I was so excited to be writing that I couldn't wait to get to my computer. Check out Julie's Vivid Living Thermometer on the next page to see my ratings for that week.

You can see that Career was a rockin' 9.5 that week – super "hot." My Environment number, however, was a 6 as my house was a bit messier than usual that week. And, my Health number was a 6. All of my workout time which keeps me feeling healthy and strong – and some of my sleep time – I spent working on my book that week. My numbers with Family and Friends dropped down a bit, too, from their normal 8, 9 or 10 status, as did time with my husband.

Yet, I gave myself a 10 for Overall Vivid Living because I consciously chose to focus my time and attention that week on the book – on my Career. It was all about my perspective and making conscious choices that week. Continuing on like that long term would definitely not have been fulfilling. So, after that week, I started to make different choices in my life to create more balance again.

Giving yourself a 9 or 10 is not claiming perfection. It is celebrating choice – your choice to create something that is "perfectly imperfect." This perspective is a glass half-full perspective. Know that even when you give yourself high ratings – 9's and 10's – there is still room for growth. You might be surprised at how easy it is to successfully make more changes and choices in your life when you live from a glass half-full vs. glass half-empty perspective.

JULIE'S VIVID LIVING THERMOMETER

Date: April 1

AREA OF YOUR LIFE	RATING 0-10
CAREER	9.5
ENVIRONMENT	6
FAMILY	7
FRIENDS	6
FUN	8
HEALTH	6
ME AS MOM	7
MONEY	7
PERSONAL GROWTH	9
SIGNIFICANT OTHER	7
SPIRITUALITY	8
OVERALL VIVID LIVING	10

AREA OF FOCUS _____

COMMITMENT _____

_____

> What's possible for you when you live your life from a glass half-full vs. a glass half-empty perspective?

Elisa's Story

Elisa, a client and mom of three living in the hustle and bustle of New York City shared her Vivid Living Thermometer ratings with me during one session. Most of her numbers were 6's or 7's. Yet she gave herself an overall Vivid Living rating of 10. I was surprised by this and became curious. Usually her overall Vivid Living rating was low – somewhere between a 3 and a 7.

She said that even though things weren't where she wanted them to be, she felt she was making progress and knew how to keep raising her ratings. Most importantly, she exclaimed that she felt proud of herself and more confident than ever.

On another call with Elisa a couple of weeks later, all of her numbers were 9's and 10's. She was still working on many of the same issues as in the prior weeks. This week she simply tapped into the perspective that even though she still had work to do in each area of the Vivid Living Thermometer, everything overall was really, really good and was moving in the right direction. The forward movement and her perspective about it gave her the space and freedom to choose 9's and 10's.

So, you can see from Elisa's example that Vivid Living is not about perfection – it is about living a life YOU design, choose and, therefore, love. Remember, no one has a perfect life. It just doesn't exist. But what you can do is live a life you consciously create. When you consciously choose and create it, then it might very well feel like a 10 – even when it isn't perfect.

> What's the difference for you between living a life of 10's on your Vivid Living Thermometer and living a perfect life?

The Ripple Effect

I assume one of the reasons you picked up this book is because you'd like to raise the ratings in one or more areas of your life. If you happen to be feeling overwhelmed by all you hope to transform then here's some glorious news. The different areas of your life flow together and are interconnected.

So, instead of feeling overwhelmed, you can focus on shifting just one area and watch as the other areas are positively affected by the ripple. When you tend to one area, no matter which one it is, all the others will transform in some way, too.

Start by simply getting curious about your ratings. Which one area are you drawn to changing first? What would it look like or feel like to raise that particular rating up one point, two points, or even all the way to a 10?

Write the name of your area here.

_____

What would that area look or feel like if you raised it up one point?

_____
_____
_____
_____

What would that area look or feel like if you raised it up two points?

_____
_____
_____
_____

What would it look like or feel like if you raised it up to a 10? _____

_____
_____
_____
_____

When you let yourself get curious about your ratings and life, you will start to notice big and little ways that things can change. When you start to transform one area of your life – even a teeny, tiny bit – you will discover that the ripples will touch and transform other areas, too.

> Think about a time in your life when you made a change in one area of your life that had a positive impact on other areas of your life.

Lili's Story

Lili, a working mother of two, realized that on her Vivid Living Thermometer, Money was "out of control" in her life. She was focused so much on balancing her family and career that Money dropped off of her radar screen. When she completed her Vivid Living Thermometer she rated Money at a 4. Lili determined that in order to increase it to a 6, she could pay her bills and family necessities first and then set up specific accounts for retirement and her children's education that would go untouched. She hadn't been doing this in the past.

When we checked in two weeks later she had taken the steps mentioned above. These concrete and simple actions raised her Money rating to a 6. The shifts in this area positively affected other areas of her life as well. Personal Growth moved from 6 to 7 as she felt like she was challenging herself to grow in new and important ways. Significant Other increased from 4 to 6 as she and her husband fought less about Money and felt more hopeful that their family would find financial stability.

Here's an example of some ripples from my life. A few weeks ago I felt exceptionally sluggish and crabby. I've learned over the years that when I feel this way it is usually because my sleep, exercise, or diet is out of whack. And, you know what? All three of them were out of whack that week.

The thought of trying to make changes in all of those departments felt way too overwhelming. So I picked one area to focus on. I committed to 10 p.m. as my bedtime. That's it. I let the other areas go.

When I slept longer, I had more energy to wake up early to work out, do some yoga, or to journal (me time). I felt healthier and stronger in my body. So, instead of shoving the first kid-snack I could get my hands on into my mouth to give me a quick pick me up, I reached for veggies and nuts. I had more patience with myself and my family. I remembered to breathe – and laugh! – more. It felt wonderful!!

From just one small shift – going to bed at 10 p.m. – so much transformed in my life.

Paying attention to your Vivid Living Thermometer ratings, getting curious about what you could shift, and then taking some action – even just picking the low hanging fruit – can and will affect other areas of your life.

You don't have to transform everything today. In fact, you can't. So, just let the ripple from one change wash over your life and see what you transform. Watch as you get closer to living your vivid and extraordinary life one ripple (or even wave) at a time.

The Ever-Changing Vivid Living Thermometer

The Vivid Living Thermometer is not static. Nothing in life ever is. There is always an ebb and flow to your daily life. The shifts and movements can be very subtle or boldly obvious. You can be sure that whether your ratings were "hot" or "not" today, your ratings will definitely shift in some way over time.

Your ratings are ever-changing, and the Vivid Living Thermometer gives you a snapshot of your life, right now, in this very moment. If you assess your life via the Vivid Living Thermometer again tomorrow or even after you finish this session, the numbers on your Vivid Living Thermometer could be different. So, don't let the numbers define or scare you.

Most of us at any given moment have areas of our life that feel better – more balanced, fuller, and richer – than other areas. This is perfectly natural. So, celebrate what is going well – I mean really celebrate it. Take yourself out to dinner, throw yourself a party, and honor any little or big bit of your life that is going well. Know that the areas that aren't so "hot" right now can and will change.

Over the next few days and weeks, I invite you to use the Vivid Living Thermometer to inspire you to get curious about what shifts and changes in your life from day to day and week to week. Use your ratings to help you to move forward. If there is flow…there is hope.

Take Your Life's Temperature to Clarify Your Main Aim

Look back at your Main Aim (your goals and intentions) from the end of your JumpStart Survey in session I. Did filling in your Vivid Living Thermometer inspire you to add to or change your Main Aim? Know that as you continue along your Vivid Living journey, grow, and gain more tools and awareness, your Main Aim may evolve. Allow yourself the freedom to change it. Nothing here is written in stone.

On the next page is a blank copy of the Main Aim. Here is space for you to revisit (or rewrite) your Main Aim to see if it is still the same as when you first completed your JumpStart Survey. Feel free to add to it or change it.

Revisit Your Main Aim. List your top three to five goals or intentions. *See if your Main Aim has changed at all now that you've completed a Vivid Living Thermometer.*

> How will having a clear Main Aim (goals and intentions) as you make your way through this book help you to live a vivid and extraordinary life you love?

MAIN AIM	SCORE 0-10 10=Most & 0=Least
1.	
2.	
3.	
4.	
5.	

Take Your Life's Temperature

SESSION HIGHLIGHTS

- The Vivid Living Thermometer is one of the most informative tools around to give you a snapshot of how fulfilling and "hot" or "not" your life is, across the board, in any given moment.

- When you regularly take your life's temperature using the Vivid Living Thermometer, you'll be able to quantitatively track your growth and progress over time.

- If you aren't quite sure where to begin to live a vivid and extraordinary life you love, then the Vivid Living Thermometer will help.

- Vivid Living is not about perfection – it is about perspective. No one has a perfect life. What you can have and what does exist is living a life YOU design, choose, and therefore, love.

- Giving yourself a 9 or 10 on a Vivid Living Thermometer is about celebrating choice – your choice to create something that is "perfectly imperfect." This can also be described as a glass half-full perspective.

- When you increase the rating in one area on your Vivid Living Thermometer, the others will be positively affected, too. This is the Ripple Effect. All areas of your life are interconnected.

- Celebrate what's going well or what's "hot" on your Vivid Living Thermometer. Know that the areas that aren't so "hot" can and will change over time.

- The Vivid Living Thermometer can help you to become clearer about your Main Aim (from your JumpStart Survey).

Head over to the Take Your Life's Temperature Journal and Action Exercises and pick a few to focus on and put into practice. Then, I'll meet you for session III.

Don't forget to check in before the next session begins with a Vivid Living Thermometer (found at the end of this and every subsequent session) to take your life's temperature and get curious about what you may have already shifted.

> Name one thing in your life that's going well in this moment (even if you wouldn't rate it at a 10). What can you do to celebrate it? Maybe celebrating is simply taking a deep breath and breathing it into your body. Maybe it's going out to dinner, jumping up and down, wrapping your arms around yourself and hugging YOU. Anything goes – just celebrate what is good right now. There is absolutely something in this moment that is good and worth celebrating.

VIVID LIVING THERMOMETER   Date _____

AREA OF YOUR LIFE	RATING 0-10
CAREER	
ENVIRONMENT	
FAMILY	
FRIENDS	
FUN	
HEALTH	
ME AS MOM	
MONEY	
PERSONAL GROWTH	
SIGNIFICANT OTHER	
SPIRITUALITY	
OVERALL VIVID LIVING	

AREA OF FOCUS _____
COMMITMENT_____

Take Your Life's Temperature

JOURNAL EXERCISES

* *Reminder: No need to do all the exercises. Focus on the one/s that excite or interest you the most.*

1. What stands out most for me about my Vivid Living Thermometer?

2. What areas of my life could use some attention or do I want to change?

3. What is more terrifying: challenging myself to transform my life or my life staying exactly the same as it is today? Why?

4. What does a life I love look like and feel like? If you aren't completely sure today, that's just fine. *The rest of this book will help you figure it out. Start with capturing whatever pops up for you – images, colors, smells, textures, visions, emotions, hopes and dreams – anything you imagine Vivid Living might look like and feel like.*

5. How am I already living a life I love?

6. What activities or ways of being in my life today get me living a 10 for even a few seconds?

7. How do I know when things are in balance or out of balance in my life?

Take Your Life's Temperature

ACTION EXERCISES

* *Reminder: No need to do all the exercises. Focus on the one/s that excite or interest you the most.*

1. **Vivid Living Thermometer Visualization**

    If you're not sure how to do a visualization then see page 21 for visualization suggestions. And, if you aren't a big fan of doing visualizations, you can still take yourself through the questions below. Just keep your eyes open.

    If you want to hear me guide you through this visualization then visit www.vividliving.net/freebookdownloads to download the **Vivid Living Thermometer Visualization Audio Recording**

    This visualization will help you get some clarity about specific actions you can take to increase the ratings on your Vivid Living Thermometer. Visualizations are great for getting you to use your mind and body together. Feel free to experiment. Don't hold yourself back and remember…there is no such thing as perfect.

    Use the blank spaces provided between questions to capture your visualization experience.

a. What one area from your Vivid Living Thermometer are you drawn to changing first? Write the name of the area here.

b. **Staying the same.** Close your eyes and take three deep breaths. Imagine the area of your life that you chose staying at the number it is at today, forever. What do you notice in your body? How do you feel? What is your life like?

c. **Up two points.** Close your eyes and take three breaths. Imagine the number for the area you chose increasing by two points. What do you notice in your body? What's different in your life? How are you different? What did you do or who were you being that helped you to raise your rating?

Write down and commit to taking at least one action to raise your rating by two points. *No need to see the whole path clearly. If it's challenging to come up with specific actions then just try* **something** *different. Depending on what area you chose to focus on, this might look like going for more walks, picking up a book on meditation and giving it a try, having dinner with a friend, going to a movie on your own, listening to music, dancing in your living room, only eating foods with ingredients that your grandma would have had in her kitchen, updating your resume, having a hard conversation that you've been putting off, getting a massage or facial, etc. Trust and believe that you'll know what it looks* *and feels like for you. Choose something that gets your blood pumping and feels exciting.*

    d. **At a 10!** Close your eyes and take three breaths. Imagine your rating at a 10. What do you notice in your body? How do you feel? What's different in your life? How are you different? What did you do or who were you being that helped you to raise your rating to a 10? *As you get closer to living a life you love or 10's on your Vivid Living Thermometer, your Ogres – or limiting thoughts and beliefs, fears, etc. (covered in more detail in session VI, "Get Those Ogres") will probably become louder and stronger. Ask them to step aside so you can get a sense of what a 10 feels like in your life and body. Let yourself really feel and experience it.*

Write down and commit to at least one action that could raise your rating to a 10. Choose an action(s) that excites, enlivens, and maybe even terrifies you. *Those feelings of terror are just Ogres popping up again – keep imagining and living into the vision and energy of a 10 and move forward anyway. No need to see the whole path clearly. Choose any action that excites or enlivens you even a little bit. If you aren't sure, just choose something to commit to as an experiment and see what shifts as a result. Maybe you sign up for a class to learn something you always dreamed of learning, go sky diving, plan a trip to bike across Italy, share a hidden truth with a family member or friend, commit to leaving an unfulfilling job, say "No!" to excess shopping, etc.*

    e. **Repeat.** Repeat the visualization above for each area of your life that wants some attention. Do something every day to consciously increase your Vivid Living Thermometer ratings.

2. **The Ripple Effect.** Focus on making just one change, even a teeny, tiny one, in one area of your life and notice the ripple… You don't have to transform everything today. In fact, you can't. So, let the ripple from one change wash over your life and see what you transform.

Use the blank spaces provided between questions to capture your thoughts and experience.

    a. **Choose it.** Choose one area of your life to focus on that could use some attention. Write it down here.

    b. **Commit and share it.** Write down or tell someone about the one commitment you are making to yourself this month to shift that area in some way. It can be a big or tiny commitment. Any kind of shift will create a ripple. Write down the name/s of the people with whom you are going to share your commitment.

    c. **Do it.** Follow through with your commitment to yourself. You can do it!

    d. **Notice it.** Set aside a time every night or once a week (e.g., Sunday nights) to consciously look back at other areas of your life. Notice the ripple effects. What are you shifting? What have you transformed? Write what you notice here.

e. **Celebrate!** Celebrate the ripples or the waves you created. Movement is good! List the different ways you can celebrate.

3. **Fill out a Vivid Living Thermometer every day.** Notice what changes for you from day to day. How did you bring about the changes?

4. **Fill in a glass half-full Vivid Living Thermometer.** Fill in your Vivid Living Thermometer from a slightly different perspective. Put your hand on your heart. Breathe. As you fill in the Vivid Living Thermometer ask yourself what the highest rating is that you could possibly give to each area of your life right now. Imagine each area of your life from a glass half-full instead of a glass half-empty perspective. What changes? What do you notice in your body when you do this? What changes do you notice in your ratings on the Vivid Living Thermometer?

> Visit www.vividliving.net/freebookdownloads to download a blank copy of the **Vivid Living Thermometer**. Feel free to share it!

What's My Homework?

Take Your Life's Temperature Session II

What actions or reflections are you committed to do, to practice, or to think about? Let these be things that interest, excite or even terrify you. Challenge yourself!

1.

2.

3.

4.

Create structures. Do you think it might be challenging for you to remember to do your homework or keep your commitments? If so, then pick out some structures to put in place to remind you of them. It's easy to get excited about your commitments and intentions. The hard part is keeping them. Structures can help.

> Look at page 24 to see the **Suggested Structures List**. Or, visit www.vividliving.net/freebookdownloads to download the **Suggested Structures List.**

Vivid Living Resources

SESSION II

FREE Digital Downloads

Vivid Living Thermometer. Download as many copies as you wish of the Vivid Living Thermometer. Feel free to share it!

www.vividliving.net/freebookdownloads

Vivid Living Thermometer Visualization Audio Recording. Is visualization new for you or sometimes challenging? Do you like being guided through visualizations? Then download this audio to hear me guide you through the Vivid Living Thermometer Visualization.

www.vividliving.net/freebookdownloads

Recommended Reading

Co-Active Coaching: New Skills For Coaching People Toward Success by Laura Whitworth, Karen Kimsey-House, Henry Kimsey-House, Phillip Sandahl.

Vivid Living Check-In

SESSION II

1. What have I learned?

2. What challenges did I run into?

3. What do I want to remember that will help me to live a vivid and extraordinary life I love?

4. Fill in a Vivid Living Thermometer today. See what's shifting for you as you journey along your Vivid Living adventure.

VIVID LIVING THERMOMETER   Date _____

AREA OF YOUR LIFE	RATING 0-10
CAREER	
ENVIRONMENT	
FAMILY	
FRIENDS	
FUN	
HEALTH	
ME AS MOM	
MONEY	
PERSONAL GROWTH	
SIGNIFICANT OTHER	
SPIRITUALITY	
OVERALL VIVID LIVING	

AREA OF FOCUS _____
COMMITMENT _____

Notes

Listen to Your BodyTruth

SESSION III

> *The mind can assert anything and pretend it has proved it.*
> *My beliefs I test on my body, on my intuitional consciousness,*
> *and when I get a response there, then I accept.*
> *Life is only bearable when the mind and the body are in harmony,*
> *and there is a natural balance between the two,*
> *and each has a natural respect for the other.*
> **D.H. Lawrence**

> *There is more wisdom in your body than in your deepest philosophies.*
> **Friedrich Nietzsche**

Did your numbers on the Vivid Living Thermometer change at all from the last session to this one? There are more tools to come that can help you to keep your high ratings high, and help to increase those low ratings.

The tool that we're going to focus in this session is a fun one – BodyTruth. When you tap into the unique wisdom and language of your body you are accessing your BodyTruth. In this session I'll show you how to recognize, listen to, and then use your powerful BodyTruth to help you live a vivid and extraordinary life you love.

Get curious about how tapping into your BodyTruth can shift the ratings on your Vivid Living Thermometer, support you in reaching your Main Aim (maybe even tweak or redefine it), and help you to make the changes you most desire.

This will be a new tool for many of you. And it is one of the most important tools in this book. The wisdom and language of your body will help you navigate through the subsequent sessions. And, it can steer you directly toward vivid and extraordinary living.

When you use your BodyTruth, you can completely alter how you make decisions and feel about yourself in your family, community, workplace, and world. The more fluent you are with using this tool, the more confident you'll feel in your busy life. You'll have access to your absolute truth. Your body doesn't lie!

Here you'll read examples of how other busy moms used their BodyTruth to make decisions about things as ordinary as what to drink in the morning and as profound as what city to call home.

Get curious and be open to what comes during this session. Know that accessing your BodyTruth may take some time and practice. Be patient and gentle with yourself. Most of all, have fun!

The Body and the Mind – Dynamic Duo

Everyone has a body. Your body keeps you alive and helps you to shape the kind of life you live. When your body is strong and healthy you are able to move through the world with physical ease. When your body is rundown or compromised, it takes increased mental, emotional, and physical effort to live each day.

In this session, you'll dive deeper than your physical health into the rich and deep ocean of the language and wisdom of your body. Most of you are probably familiar with the language and voices in your mind. If your mind is anything like mine, then it is on, working and talking, often very loudly, 24/7. Did you know that your body has its own voice and language, too?

> What are some ways that your body talks to you? *Think about how you know when you are tired, hungry, angry, happy, sad, etc.*

Once you can access the language and wisdom of your body, you can bring it together with all of the wisdom in your mind. When your mind and body are working together in harmony, you'll feel confident and clear, and you'll have more trust in yourself and your decisions than you ever imagined.

Much of my coaching work focuses on helping clients uncover the rich wisdom and language of their bodies – their BodyTruth. I'm going to share how I do that with you in this session. We'll focus on how to bring your mind and your body together in subsequent sessions. In this session, however, your body has the spotlight.

Your Body Doesn't Lie

Your body has a language of its own – a language spoken in sensations, not words. Your body talks to you and gives you information every second about the world around you, what you feel, your truth, and your life. It doesn't lie.

Think about your own very young babies or children. They are wonderful examples of beings tapped into their pristine BodyTruth. It is their BodyTruth that tells babies to cry when they are hungry and to close their eyes and sleep, no matter where they are, when they are tired. As children get a bit older they blurt out what they think and feel unabashedly. They are living and speaking from their BodyTruth. Their minds filter few or none of the impulses, messages, and language they receive from their body. What they sense, they then say or act upon.

From an early age, many of us were taught to override or even to ignore the language of our body. Think back for yourself. As a child do you ever remember feeling apprehensive about shaking hands with a person that you just met and got a strange vibe from? Did your parents (with the best of intentions) push you to shake hands anyway to be polite? This may have started to teach you about the conventions of society – definitely important knowledge to have. At the same time, somewhere in there, you may have lost the ability to trust or hear your BodyTruth.

As an adult, have you ever made a big decision (or even a little one) based on something you thought you **should** do instead of something you **wanted** to do? Have you convinced yourself in your mind that you'd be happy or could make something that didn't quite feel right, work? Only to realize later it wasn't quite the best move for you? Maybe you let the voices in your mind override the language and knowing in your body.

> Think of a time when you did something because you thought you **should** do it, not because you actually **wanted** to do. Think of a time when you did something purely because you **wanted** to. What is the difference for you between the times when you think you **should** do something versus the times when you **want** to do something?

Suzanne's Story

Suzanne is a passionate and energetic newly married woman excited to one day start her own family, open her own business (a clothing boutique), and move to the East Coast to be close to family. She wasn't quite sure where to start to make it all happen, so she dove into some individual coaching.

From the very first session I introduced her to her BodyTruth. By our fifth session, she realized she has always known her truth but hasn't always listened. She told me about when she moved to Chicago (where she currently lives) and had a pit in her stomach the whole time. She ignored it, pushed it aside, and moved to Chicago anyway.

During our work together Suzanne realized she had not been listening to her BodyTruth – the natural wisdom she had right with her always (e.g., the knowledge that Chicago is not the city for her). She is now creating new and exciting plans that include moving to the East Coast with her husband in the next nine months, starting her business online, and, most significantly, starting a family. Tapping into and using her BodyTruth helped her design and live a vivid and extraordinary life she's excited about.

Being present in the moment with what you experience in your body is absolutely the first step to Vivid Living. By practicing and using the tools from this session, you will start to recognize the sensations in your body when you are living a vivid life you love, living a mediocre life, or just doggone livin' a rotten life. Once you know the difference, you get to choose, more consciously than ever, the kind of life you want to live.

Sensations vs. Feelings

Your body speaks in sensations instead of words. When you listen and pay close attention you can decipher a wide and beautiful range of sensations. Many people confuse sensations with feelings. **Sensations and feelings are not the same thing.**

Merriam Webster's dictionary defines a feeling as, "an emotional state or reaction." A feeling is a great example of how powerful it is when the mind and body work together. The sensations in your body paired with your beliefs about those sensations are what create your feelings. Many of you can name your feelings, but you may have a hard time deciphering the underlying sensations that led you to those feelings in the first place.

When we try to describe sensations, we can do so with words, sounds, colors, images, or movement. Each sensation can vary in terms of intensity, frequency, and mobility.

Here are a few words to help you to describe some of your sensations.

Cold	Flow	Shaking
Hot	Looseness	Soft
Pressure	Flushed	Hard

Tension	Open	Pleasure
Tightness	Prickly	Pain

Each of us has a unique way of experiencing emotions in our body. The sensations one person notices in his/her body might be totally different from what another person experiences. Below, you can see how Tina, a mom of two, experienced stress and joy in her body. Your own experience of these emotions may be similar to Tina's or completely different.

Tina's Story

Tina shared with her Vivid Living Coaching Group that when she imagined feeling stressed in Los Angeles traffic her heart began to race. It was hard to breathe and her head hurt.

When Tina remembered a joyful time, finishing her PhD, she noticed her heart swell, her body lift up, and her breath expand.

> What sensations are you noticing right now? What feelings are you feeling right now?

Cheryl's Story

After doing the exercises in this session and focusing on the sensations in her body for a week, Cheryl, a mom of two young boys, found out just how powerful it could be to slow down and pay attention to her body. During the week she became acutely aware of how her ritual morning cup of coffee left her feeling energized (which she liked) and also tingly and jittery (which she didn't like). She had never paid attention to the more subtle effects that coffee had on her body until now.

When she paid attention to the unique language of her body she understood that morning coffee wasn't for her. She didn't want to lose her energizing morning boost and found a compromise. She now drinks tea in the morning for her calmer and gentler energy boost. Occasionally, she'll drink coffee in the afternoon, which she noticed doesn't give her the same tingles and jitters as her morning cup. *She felt empowered and proud of her creative choice thanks to slowing down and paying attention to her sensations – her BodyTruth.*

Don't Fix It. Notice It.

Some of you may find it uncomfortable to feel too much emotion – be it too sad or even too happy. We may focus our life-energy on monitoring, muting, managing, changing, or even eradicating our feelings. In fact, what we are really trying to mange are the sensations we experience in our body when we feel a certain emotion.

Have you ever felt so excited (so much energy in your body) that you wanted to jump up and down, but didn't let yourself? What's it like when you hold yourself back? Is it hard to contain – like something (energy) gets stuck in your body? It takes a lot of life energy to control our natural impulses. In fact, it often takes more energy to contain them than it would have taken to actually just jump up and down in the first place.

Now, I'm not suggesting that you need to jump up and down for joy every moment you feel that impulse. That's just not practical. Simply noticing and naming the impulse is a great first step. Then you can choose how and when you do let sensations or energy flow and move through your body.

Once you trust that you can handle any and all sensations that come your way (after all they are only one part of you, not all of you) then you can begin to free trapped and previously inaccessible energy. Once you can access this energy, you can then use it to create a vivid life you love instead of a muted life that you just like or tolerate.

Remind yourself that you can handle any and all sensations in your body. There is nothing to be scared of – it is just YOU. The key is to simply notice and be with whatever sensations are present for you in any given moment. This in itself will shift and change those sensations eventually. When you stop tying up precious energy trying to manage your sensations, then you can use that amazing energy to experience Vivid Living.

> What sensations or impulses do you sometimes experience in your body that are hard or scary for you? *Example: Some people have a hard time being with tears welling in their eyes. Some people have a hard time when they notice their body getting tight such as instinctively making a fist.* What meaning do you then make of these sensations? *Example: Some people associate anger with their tight body or with making a fist.*

Andrea's Story

Andrea, a fun and spunky writer and executive in the entertainment business, shared her experience of using the wisdom of her body with her Vivid Living Coaching Group. "I have quit smoking, again, recently. I've become really aware of my breathing and body. In the process of quitting smoking this time, I've become aware of what sensations arise in my body when I'm having a craving. I breathe and observe what it's like and say 'Oh, that's what a craving feels like and this is where it is in my body right now.' This has really helped me to keep myself from smoking this week. It's like the noticing has helped me to move from moment to moment without needing to act on every feeling, sensation, impulse, or craving. Before, if I was feeling anxious about not having a cigarette, I'd head on out to buy a pack and would get myself a cigarette to take away the anxiety. Now, instead, I'm present in my body. I notice what a craving feels like and I can even notice how it passes by just being with it. Then I notice how proud I am of myself and of being so present in my body."

Noticing and being present to your sensations can be a powerful way to release the stuck, old, and stale patterns and energy to make room for the bold, passionate, and powerful YOU!

Your Breath – The Direct Highway to Your Body

The way you access or connect to your BodyTruth is through your breath. You can tune into the language of your body (your sensations) much like you do a radio station. First, you cut through all of the static, noise, and other stations to find the one that is playing the music that you want to hear. Slowing down and breathing consciously guides you though the distractions in your life and gives you complete access to the language of your body. You can literally tune into your sensations and your absolute truth.

You can even try it right now. You are probably so busy reading and trying to make sense of the words, concepts, and ideas on this page that you aren't very tuned into what is happening right now in your body. After you read this sentence close your eyes. Take five breaths and notice whatever it is that you notice in your body. Did you notice, as I did, that with each breath it became easier and easier to notice sensations in your body? I felt my ribs expand with each breath, my shoulders lowered down, and my belly softened a bit each time I breathed.

Anna's Story

Anna, a working mom with two school-aged girls, discovered the power of her breath on one of our coaching calls. She explained to me that she felt stuck and deflated because her business wasn't growing. We had been working together for about four weeks. Anna felt really excited and enlivened by the first few weeks of coaching and then her old negative thoughts and patterns began to return.

I asked her to slow down, breathe, and name the sensations she was experiencing. She took some breaths and then noticed for the first time, a twisting and tightening in her stomach.

I reminded her to breathe right into the sensations in her stomach. She did and after about a minute or so she told me that the twisting and tightening had loosened up. She felt relaxed, could breathe more easily, and felt like a cloud had lifted from her. She was finally able to remember and feel, once again, the hope, excitement, and aliveness that she tapped into during the first few weeks of coaching. She did this not by pushing away her stuck feelings but by slowing down, breathing, naming the sensations, and being right with them.

> What feels stuck in your life? Where do you notice that "stuckness" the most in your body? If you aren't sure that's OK. Be open and curious. It will get easier to notice over time. What do you notice when you sit with the "stuckness" without trying to push it away, ignore it or change it?

Your HeartTruth!

Your BodyTruth comes from noticing sensations in your body. The sensations you notice in your stomach when you think about that upcoming parent-teacher conference alert you that something exciting or nerve-wracking is on the horizon. The sensations in your head after you've been up way too late paying bills lets you know that your brain is tired and it's time to get some sleep. The sensations in your legs after running a 5K might let you know that you'd feel wonderful if you could stretch or just sit down.

You now know that your whole body holds powerful information for you if you just slow down, breathe, and listen. There is one part of your body, however, that can tap you right in to your core and truth in an instant – your heart.

Not only is your heart is an incredibly important organ in your body, it also has been referred to as the emotional, moral, and spiritual nucleus of a human being. It is most often associated with love, compassion, and even wisdom.

You are tapping into your HeartTruth when you connect to your heart, notice the sensations there, listen to any words or messages that come to mind, or notice any images.

You access your HeartTruth in the same way you do your BodyTruth. You use your breath to help you slow down and then focus on your heart. You simply notice the sensations in the front and the back of your heart (chest) area. Most likely you'll know that you are on to some version of your HeartTruth when you notice opening, flow, aliveness, fullness, depth, light, ease, etc.

Nora's Story

Nora, a mom of two young children living in New York City, was once a successful business executive. She loved the title, status, and income that came with her job. But she was fed up with the long hours, corporate environment, and politics her job required her to navigate.

After much soul searching and some coaching, Nora finally took the plunge into full-time motherhood. This was not an easy transition for Nora. Even today she still has moments and days when she doubts her decisions and choices.

During a recent Advanced Coaching Group call, Nora shared with the group that she was again plagued by doubts and fears that she was making the wrong decision to be at home with her children. She felt confident as a business woman and clearly knew who she was in that role. She was worried that she wouldn't be a good enough mom, worried about what others would think of her, worried that she sold out, and worried she was basically just being a spoiled princess by being at home instead of working at an outside job.

I asked her to close her eyes, take a few breaths, and put her hand on her heart. When she did this she said that she immediately felt her body relax and her heart stop racing one hundred miles a minute.

Next I guided her to her HeartTruth. I asked her to check in with her heart to see what her heart knew about being a stay-at-home mom.

These are the words that came to her — the words that seemed to come from her heart, core, and a deep place of truth: "I can do it and I LOVE being with my kids. I am a great mom and want to be with them for these precious moments of childhood. I wouldn't give it up for the world, and I love my freedom."

She shared that she noticed a solidness, flow, ease, and relaxation in her whole body when she listened to the truth in her heart. Her heart felt warm, alive, full, and vibrant. She knew it was on to something true!

Checking in with the wisdom and truth in her heart enables Nora to live each day with confidence in her decision. This is especially reassuring for her as the decision to leave behind a very successful career wasn't anything she thought she'd ever choose for herself.

Nora is living with more freedom and confidence than she ever imagined. She keeps coming back to her HeartTruth whenever she has moments of doubt.

Make Body Decisions Daily

Once you can tap into the language of your body you can use it to help you make many decisions – big and little – about how you want to live your life and what it will take to live a vivid life YOU love. I'll walk you through how to make Body Decisions yourself in the Action Exercises section (Make Body Decisions, exercise 3) at the end of this session.

Here's an example of a time when I made a Body Decision. I was on a walk one day in my neighborhood. I was heading back home when I got curious and decided to check in with my body. I breathed and introduced the option of going back home to my body. Surprisingly, my body immediately tensed up and it got harder to breathe. I then tried on the option of going for a longer walk around the block again. My limbs then got heavy and tired.

It was clear to me that neither option felt enlivening or "right" in my body. So I got creative and introduced the option of standing in front of my house and doing some gentle stretches before heading inside. I noticed a lightness, freedom, energy flow, and excitement in my body. I finally found the right option for myself in that moment. I never would have thought to stop and stretch if I hadn't slowed down enough to get curious about and listen to the wisdom and language of my body.

Lisa's Story

Here is an example of how a client, Lisa, a working mom with a four-year-old daughter, used her body to change the flow and dynamics of her evenings at home.

Lisa, upon coming home from 10-hour days at the office, felt compelled to check her Blackberry five or six times every night just in case some important work messages arrived. She was constantly stressed and felt guilty that she wasn't giving her daughter and family her undivided attention.

By breathing and checking in with her sensations, she realized that each time she checked her Blackberry she experienced tightness in her chest and it was hard for her to take a deep breath. She felt jittery. When she imagined turning off her Blackberry the minute she arrived home, and focusing solely on her daughter, herself, and her husband, she noticed that her whole body relaxed. She felt free and a smile spread across her face. Wanting to feel more relaxed and at ease in the evenings with her family, she accepted the challenge of turning off her Blackberry the minute she walked in the door. It wasn't easy at first, but she practiced it until it felt easy and natural to her.

Joli's Story

Here is an example of how paying attention to the sensations and language of her body helped Joli to make a big decision in her life.

Joli, a mom of two living in a suburb of Chicago, received the good news that her husband was being considered for a substantially better paying, and better positioned job. The bad news was that it was in Texas. Joli, who loved her life in Chicago, was almost paralyzed trying to weigh the choice of staying in Chicago with a life, friends, and family that she loved, or moving to Texas for an exciting, better paying, lifestyle-enhancing, extremely rewarding job opportunity for her husband.

Joli decided her mind alone wasn't getting her closer to making a peaceful decision. She then remembered to look to her body. She closed her eyes, took some breaths and then imagined her family staying in Chicago. She paid attention to the sensations in her body. She noticed tightness in her chest and arms and that it was hard for her to breathe fully.

She then cleared away those sensations and imagined herself moving to Texas. She felt open and lighter. More energy flowed in her chest and belly and she could breathe with ease and openness.

Tapping into the wisdom of her body didn't end the decision-making process for her. What she did get, however, was more peace and clarity around how freeing, opening, and exciting the move to Texas actually could be for her. This was surprising for her, yet at the same time, it felt true and right. When she was initially stuck in her feelings of sadness, loss, and feeling overwhelmed, there was no room for her to experience the freedom and excitement that this opportunity naturally offered. In the end, she and her family decided to move to Texas.

You can use the wisdom of your body to help you figure out something as mundane as what to eat for dinner or as profound as where you want to live. Your body has its own knowledge and wisdom and is an ally of yours. Use it to help you make decisions in your life. Your body wants to speak to you and has so much to share. Your mind doesn't have to figure it all out alone.

> What's possible for you when you imagine using your BodyTruth and your mind together to help you make a decision?

Listen to Your BodyTruth

SESSION HIGHLIGHTS

- Once you can access the rich language and wisdom of your body – your BodyTruth – you can align it with the wisdom in your mind. When the mind and the body are working together in harmony, you will feel confident, clear, and you'll have more trust in yourself and your decisions than you ever imagined.

- **Your body doesn't lie.**

- Your body has a language of its own – a language spoken in sensations, not words. Your body talks to you and gives you information every second about the world around you, what you feel, your truth, and your life.

- Many people confuse sensations with feelings. They are not the same thing. Your sensations (i.e., what you experience in your body like hot, cold, tingly, tight, relaxed, etc.) paired with your beliefs about those sensations are what create your feelings.

- Noticing, naming, and being present to your sensations can be a powerful and important way to release stuck and stale energy and make room for the bold, passionate, and powerful YOU!

- The primary way you access or connect to your BodyTruth is through your breath. Slowing down and breathing consciously guides you to find your way though the distractions in your life.

- There is one part of your body that will get you right to your core – your heart. When you connect to your heart, notice the sensations there, listen to any words/messages that come to mind, or notice any images you see. This is your HeartTruth.

- Once you can tap into the language of your body you can use it to help you make many decisions, big and little, about how you want to live your life and what it will take to live a vivid life YOU love.

- Your body wants to speak to you and has so much to share. Your mind doesn't have to figure it all out alone.

I invite you to play with the Journal and Action Exercises at the end of this session to start to train your breath and mind to listen to your amazingly wise body. In no time, you'll be using your body as a tool to make choices and decisions in your life from a place of rock solid certainty and confidence. Be playful and curious. See what comes and enjoy getting to know your body in what may very well be a new and different way.

Know that it takes time and practice to learn to tap into, understand, and then use your BodyTruth. So, if this sounds hard or foreign to you, hang in there. Keep holding the intention that you'd like to get to know the language of your body better. With time and practice you absolutely will. You'll get more practice as you use your body (and your mind) in the sessions to come.

Listen to Your Body Truth

BREATH WORK

> Visit www.vividliving.net/freebookdownloads to hear me personally guide you through five of these breathing exercises in the **BodyTruth Breath Work Audio Recording.**
>
> Want a breathing reminder? Then download the **Breath Work Quick Reference Guide** at www.vividliving.net/freebookdownloads. Hang it up, put it in your car, or post it up as a screen saver. Have instant access to Breath Work anytime.

Each of the breathing exercises below will help you to tap into the sensations and language of your body and your BodyTruth. Infusing more conscious breathing into your life can help you feel calmer, more relaxed, and more focused.

When you initially practice the breathing exercises below, I encourage you to close your eyes and sit with your feet flat on the floor or lay in a comfortable position with legs and arms uncrossed. This will help you to block out distractions from the world around you and focus more deeply inside.

Once you are familiar with these breathing exercises you can do most of them while waiting in line at the grocery store, while on hold, while walking, while parked at a red light, while doing dishes, while exercising, or anytime you could use a little pick-me-up or slow-me-down.

1. **The Slow Breath.** Close your eyes and take three slow breaths. Notice the sensations in your body without judging them. Just notice them.

2. **Four-Count Breath**. On your inhale slowly count to four. On your exhale slowly count to four.

3. **Breath Count**. Take ten breaths while counting in your mind. Say each number to yourself throughout the entire inhale and exhale. When you get distracted or lose track of what number you are on, gently bring yourself back to number one and begin again.

4. **Intention Breath**. Choose two words that are meaningful for you. It might be an intention, something you love, or just something that you like thinking about that brings you joy. Say one word as you inhale and one word as you exhale. Repeat for three to five minutes.

5. **Curious Breath**. As you breathe normally notice the quality of your breath without trying to change a thing. Is your breath deep, shallow, short, long, smooth, or choppy? What parts of your body move when you breathe and what parts stay still? Just notice without any judgment for five minutes.

6. **Sound & Movement Breath**. Take six breaths. During the first two exhales let out a sound – any sound that comes to you. With the next two breaths, do any kind of movement that feels good to you during each inhale and exhale. With the next two breaths do both – make a sound and move in any way you wish. Repeat until you feel finished.

7. **Get Present Breath**. Take a few breaths. When you are ready, bring your attention to your thoughts and notice them without trying to get rid of or change any of them. Just notice them. Next, when you are ready, bring your attention to your emotions. Notice what emotions are present for you in this exact moment without any judgment or trying to change them. Then, when you are ready, bring your attention to the sensations in your body.

Notice what sensations are present for you in this exact moment. Just notice. Do you feel pressure, tightness, tension, heat, cold, tingling, loose, or flow? Be with what is present for you in this moment.

8. **Clear Mind/Don't Know Breath**. As you inhale focus on these words and say to yourself, "Clear mind, clear mind, clear mind." On your exhale, focus on and say to yourself, "Don't know." *This breathing exercise was influenced by Zen teachings.*

Listen to Your BodyTruth

JOURNAL EXERCISES

* *Reminder: No need to do all the exercises. Focus on the one/s that excite or interest you the most.*

1. **Sensation Visualization** – Begin to decipher the beautiful and powerful language of your body. Then write about what you notice in the spaces provided on pages 93-94.

   If you're not sure how to do a visualization, see page 21 for visualization suggestions.

   > Visit www.vividliving.net/freebookdownloads if you'd like to hear me guide you through this powerful **Sensation Visualization.**

   a. **Breathe and relax**. Close your eyes and choose a breathing exercise from the Breath Work section on pages 89-91 to help you get centered and solid. *If you aren't so into visualizations, you can still take yourself through the steps and questions below. Just keep your eyes open.*

   b. **Imagine and notice**. Then, when you are ready, think about a time when you felt stressed. Imagine, see, and really experience yourself feeling stressed. Bring your attention to the sensations in your body. What do you notice in your head, face, shoulders, chest, arms, back, belly, hips, and legs? What is your breathing like? Notice whatever it is that you experience in your body and welcome it all.

c. **Breathe and release**. Breathe and release that emotion and experience from your mind and body. Maybe imagine it being washed away by waves or physically shake your arms and legs to release it.

d. **Repeat**. Repeat with the following three emotions – joyful, angry, and loving to construct a reliable baseline to begin to decipher the beautiful and powerful language of your body. From here, feel free to repeat using any other emotions you wish.

If it is hard for you to perceive sensations then just stay with the emotion and write down whatever it is that you did notice – feelings, images, colors, sounds, smells, memories, and thoughts. Don't give up. It will get easier and easier with time.

Write here about what you noticed in your body when you felt…

…stressed

…joyful

…angry

...loving

...other feelings

2. **Body Postures.** Position yourself in different body postures and then write about what sensations arise in your body.

    a. **Sit hunched.** Sit hunched over. Breathe. Write about what you notice.

    b. **Sit straight.** Sit up straight with your feet flat on the floor and your body relaxed. Breathe. Write about what you notice.

    c. **Curl up**. Curl up in a fetal position. Breathe. Write about what you notice.

d. **Stand straight**. Stand up straight. Breathe. Write about what you notice.

e. **Other postures**. Try on any other postures that you are curious about. Write about what you notice.

3. **Tap into your HeartTruth**. Use your breath to help you slow down and focus on your heart. Then notice the sensations in the front and the back of your heart (chest) area. Listen for any words of wisdom or images that pop into your mind. Most likely you'll know you are onto some version of your HeartTruth when you experience opening, flow, aliveness, fullness, depth, light, ease, etc.

   a. **Name it**. Write down a question, fear, or doubt you have in your life.

b. **Breathe**. Close your eyes and take three breaths. Maybe even do a breathing exercise from the Breath Work section on pages 89-91.

c. **Hand on heart**. Once you feel ready, put your hand onto your heart. Feel your hand on your heart and your heart underneath your hand.

d. **Ask your heart**. Now, ask your heart what it knows about the question, fear, or doubt.

e. **Listen and notice**. Notice the sensations in your heart, any messages that you hear in your head, or any images that pop into your mind. *Most people hear their HeartTruth in words. But, sometimes images, colors, smells, or sensations arise that hold some meaning. Go with whatever comes up for you. Trust your heart and trust yourself. There is no right or wrong way to do this.*

f. **Write it**. Capture and write about (or even draw) your HeartTruth here.

4. **Talk with your HeartTruth**. Here you get to have a conversation with your HeartTruth. Yes, you actually can talk with your HeartTruth. Some people might call it talking with their inner "spirit" or "guide." I call it talking with your HeartTruth. Feel free to give it a different name if that works better for you. It is most powerful to write as you do this exercise. But you can also do this in your head when you don't have any pen or paper handy.

a. Take a few breaths and put your hand on your heart as you breathe to help you tap into the wisdom of your heart.

b. Write your name on the paper with a colon after it as though you are writing the dialogue for a play. Then write down the first question you have for your HeartTruth. *Example:* **Julie:** *When will I be done writing the manuscript for this book?*

(Your Name) _____

(Write your question here.)

_____

c. Write down HeartTruth and place a colon after it. Then write down whatever you hear your HeartTruth say to you.

Example: **HeartTruth:** *In January.*

HeartTruth:

d. Continue this process and dialogue as long as it feels right for you.

Example: **Julie:** *Are you kidding me? That's so soon. How in the world am I going to get it done by January?*

HeartTruth: *You will find a way. It will be finished by then.*

Julie: *How will I know when it is finished?*

HeartTruth: *You will know. You'll feel it in your mind and body. You will be certain.*

Julie: *What do I need to do now to get it done?*

HeartTruth: *Just keep writing word by word, one day at a time, breathe and you will get it done. Trust and believe in yourself.*

(Your Name) _____

HeartTruth:

_____

(Your Name) _____

HeartTruth:

_____

e. When you are done with your conversation, make sure that you thank your HeartTruth for sharing its wisdom with you and say whatever else you wish to say in order to bring the conversation to a close.

Example: ***Julie:*** *Thank you for sharing your wisdom with me today. I look forward to more… Thanks and Love, Julie*

(Your Name):

Listen to Your BodyTruth

ACTION EXERCISES

* *Reminder: No need to do all the exercises. Focus on the one/s that excite or interest you the most.*

1. **Practice Breath Work**. Practice one different type of breathing exercise from the Breath Work section on pages 89-91 every day for 3-10 minutes.

2. **Every day notice at least one time when:**

    a. You do something, think something, or engage in behavior that creates the sensations in your body that you want to experience more often. Write them here.

    Example: *When I go for a walk at lunch I feel tingling and energy flow in my body.*

    b. You do something, think something, or engage in behavior that gives you the sensations in your body that you don't want to experience or don't serve you. Write them here.

    Example: *When I ran that yellow light I felt jittery, a rush of adrenaline, and tightness in my chest and breath.*

3. **Make Body Decisions**. Once a day use your body to help you make a Body Decision following the steps below. The decision can be small, like, "Do I want mint chocolate chip, cookie dough, coffee, or vanilla ice cream?" Or, the decision can be big, like, "Do I want to live in San Diego or New York City?"

    a. **The decision**. Think about one decision you want to make and write it down. State it as clearly as possible. The decision can be about anything. Example: *I want to decide how to act with my overbearing in-laws.*

    b. **Possibilities list.** Come up with a list of ALL the different possibilities. Don't censor yourself. *Example: Even if you think you must be cheerful to your in-laws, allow yourself to play with the option to never talk to them again. When you invite in all the options as viable possibilities, you then give yourself the true freedom of choice.*

    c. **Breathe.**

    d. **Imagine each option.**

        i.   When you are centered, solid, and ready, imagine yourself doing and living the first option.

        ii. Breathe. Notice what happens in your body.

        iii. Breathe and release the first option.

        iv. When you are centered, solid, and ready, imagine yourself doing and living the second option.

        v.   Breathe. Notice what happens in your body.

vi. Repeat as necessary until you've tried on all options and noticed the effect of each option in your body.

   e. **Use it**. Use this information to help inform your decision making process. Did any option excite or enliven you? Did you notice calm, ease, or deeper breaths when you imagined an option? Did any option make you smile?

   f. **Practice.** The more you do this the easier it will be to tap into your body to make any kind of big or small decision in your life.

4. **Change your body posture**. Catch yourself sitting or standing in a way that gives you sensations in your body that you don't want. Change your posture (maybe even your breath) to create sensations that you do want.

5. **Give yourself a pick-me-up**. Take a few breaths and envision a time when you felt joyful, peaceful, loving, etc. See that time in your mind's eye and let yourself drink it in and soak it into your body and cells as if you were there again. What do you notice in your body when you do this? Do this anytime you want a pick-me-up.

What's My Homework?

LISTEN TO YOUR BODYTRUTH SESSION III

What actions or reflections are you committed to do, to practice, or to think about? Let these be things that interest, excite, or even terrify you. Challenge yourself!

1.

2.

3.

4.

Create structures. Do you think it might be challenging for you to remember to do your homework or keep your commitments? If so, then pick out some structures to put in place to remind you of them. It's easy to get excited about your commitments and intentions. The hard part is keeping them. Structures can help.

> Look at page 24 to see the **Suggested Structures List.** Or, visit www.vividliving.net/freebookdownloads to download the **Suggested Structures List.**

Vivid Living Resources

SESSION III

FREE Digital Downloads

⬇ **BodyTruth Breath Work Audio Recording.** I'll personally guide you through five of the breathing exercises in this session. Download the audio to your phone or computer and listen to it whenever you want a little pick-me-up or slow-me-down.

www.vividliving.net/freebookdownloads

⬇ **Breath Work Quick Reference Guide.** Want to remember to breathe more? Then download this Quick Reference Guide and hang it up, put it in your bag, car, or post it up as a screen saver. Have instant access to Breath Work anytime.

www.vividliving.net/freebookdownloads

⬇ **Sensation Visualization Audio Recording.** Download this audio to hear me guide you through the Sensation Visualization. Connect to and begin to decipher the powerful language of your body.

www.vividliving.net/freebookdownloads

Recommended Reading

Body-Centered Coaching: Using the Body as a Resource for Change by Marlena Field

Find Your Inner Voice by Karol Ward

Only Don't Know: Selected Teaching Letters by Seung Sahn

Three Minute Meditator by David Harp

Vivid Living Check-In

SESSION III

1. What have I learned?

2. What challenges did I run into?

3. What do I want to remember that will help me to live a vivid and extraordinary life I love?

4. Fill in a Vivid Living Thermometer today. See what's shifting for you as you journey along your Vivid Living adventure.

VIVID LIVING THERMOMETER   Date _____

AREA OF YOUR LIFE	RATING 0-10
CAREER	
ENVIRONMENT	
FAMILY	
FRIENDS	
FUN	
HEALTH	
ME AS MOM	
MONEY	
PERSONAL GROWTH	
SIGNIFICANT OTHER	
SPIRITUALITY	
OVERALL VIVID LIVING	

AREA OF FOCUS _____
COMMITMENT_____

Notes

Get to Your Core

SESSION IV

> *We all have the extraordinary coded within us,*
> *waiting to be released.*
> **Jean Houston**

> *It takes courage to grow up and turn out to be*
> *who you really are.*
> **e.e. cummings**

So you've got the Vivid Living Thermometer under your belt. You're practicing using the language of your body to help you tap into your truth. Now, we're going to uncover your Essences – who you are at your core.

I'll bet a lot has changed for you since becoming a mom. You now have children, maybe even a life partner, and your days are probably pretty different from those before being a mom. At some point during motherhood, many moms face the need to reevaluate what is most important to them. The things that used to be *important to you or excited you may no longer be relevant in your life. Your priorities have probably changed. The landscape of motherhood, with all of its beauty and challenges, has a way of shifting so much in our lives.*

What probably hasn't changed, however, is who you are at your core. You may not know fully who you are in there. That's OK! I'll bet you've had moments (if only for a few seconds) in your life that feel absolutely right, true, solid, and resonant. In this session you'll have a chance to build on what you already know about yourself. I'll walk you through the steps you need to take to uncover your unique core Essences.

I encourage you to keep listening to your BodyTruth throughout this session. Your body holds much information for you. If accessing the language of your body is still challenging, don't worry. Just keep practicing, and be curious. You'll get it eventually. Let's dive into your core!

What's an Essence?

When I was a coaching client, from the very beginning I knew there was more for me than the stagnant, fear-ridden life I was leading. I looked around and saw the passion, peace, and confidence enjoyed by so many others. I wanted it, too. I knew I could have it. I just wasn't sure how to get it.

Then, my coach introduced me to the idea of **Essences – who you are, uniquely and intrinsically, at your core – the things that make you the real YOU.** Once I could name and define my Essences, I used them as a guide to answer any and every big or little life question that landed before me. I simply had to ask myself if what I was contemplating or choosing would take me closer to or further away from my Essences.

Here's an example of something I was mulling over about the time I was first introduced to coaching. I was engaged to be married. I knew I loved my fiancé, Ken (now my husband), but I was curious about how to really know if he was "the one." Uncovering and fully living into and honoring my top Essences gave me all the information I needed to trust myself and my instincts!

My Essences didn't say to me, "Yes, Ken is the one!" Essences don't do that. They guided me in a subtle and powerful way to do the things that brought the most joy and aliveness into my life. They guided me to be the person I am at my core – unmistakably. Over time, and with practice, I became a master at infusing my everyday life with my Essences. I no longer felt unsure about who I was and what was important to me. When I honored my Essences, I felt ignited with life, confidence, peace, and excitement in every cell of my body.

Over time it was clear to me that the life Ken and I were creating together supported me to live more fully than ever into all of my Essences. This, in turn, helped me to know with confidence that I was on the right path with the right person – the person I wanted to share my life and grow old with!

The table on the following page offers additional information about Essences: what they are and what they are not. You'll begin to see that you can tell in your body, mind, and life when you're actually living into them.

> What would shift in your life if you knew, without a doubt, who you are at your core?

What Essences Are and Are Not

Essences are…	**Essences are not…**
Who you are in your heart and core.	Who you would like, should, or ought to be.
What makes you uniquely you.	Who others think you should be.
What is essential to your being.	About character or ethics.
Guides that help you make decisions in your life.	Things or activities (money, gardening).
Intangible.	Found in your head.
You know you are not living into your Essences when…	**You know you are living into your Essences when…**
You feel stuck.	You are excited to live each day.
You are in your head.	Your life is fulfilling.
It feels like you are going against the grain.	You live in a way that is truly inspiring to you.
Discord is a constant in your life.	Decisions are clear and outcomes fulfilling even when it's "hard" or "scary."
You struggle to make the "right" decision.	You know you have many choices in your life.
You make decisions based on what is easiest (most comfortable) in the moment.	You sense flow, energy and aliveness in your body and life.
You sense heaviness, deadness, and stuckness in your life and body.	

Essences vs. Values

Without your core Essences you absolutely wouldn't be YOU. Essences are **not** values. A value is a principle, standard, or quality considered worthwhile or desirable. A value is typically something you think is important to you because of the influence of family, religion, or society. Although your values may be very important to you now, they may change over time or with external influence.

You may hold a value that also happens to be an Essence. There are times, however, when people adopt values not truly in line with what is most important to them at their core. They think they "should" be or feel a particular way, but the feeling isn't necessarily guided by their truth or what they most desire.

One mom came to me holding a strong value of Accomplishment. She believed or learned over time that she isn't truly worthwhile unless she achieved significant professional accomplishments for which she was recognized. Most things in her life revolved around this value. In her heart, though, she knew her accomplishments weren't what mattered most.

Through our coaching work together, she uncovered that what was more important to her than Accomplishment was her Essence of *Adventure/Challenge*. It really didn't matter to her if others recognized her as long as she lived on her edge, challenged herself, and learned and did things that excited her and made her feel alive.

By identifying this Essence, she shifted her life energy away from Accomplishment seeking and toward *Adventure/Challenge* seeking. These are things that make her feel the most excited, and challenged – the most HER.

An Essence has little to do with what you (or anyone else for that matter) **thinks** is important. When you uncover your Essences, stay away from what you **think** is considered worthwhile or desirable. Instead, dig deep to uncover who YOU are at your core.

You might have guessed that **your body and not your mind** will guide you most directly and easily to your Essences. You may know you have hit on a true Essence when you feel solid, alive, tingling, and grounded in your body.

Live Your Essences Each and Every Day

Once you uncover and define your core Essences, your homework will be to practice honoring and living into them as often as possible – every day. As you increasingly live into your Essences, you will automatically find yourself living a life that feels satisfying, fun, and exciting. Your confidence will soar. You'll feel excited to wake up in the morning, and you'll feel more balanced. You'll have absolute clarity around what is most important to you. You'll find even more strength and courage to be that extraordinary, bold, and beautiful mama that you are.

When I say live into your Essences every day I don't mean that if one of your core Essences happens to be *Adventure* that you have to go out and bungee jump every day. You can live into your Essences in gigantic or teeny tiny ways. The goal is to awaken the energy of the Essence in you – in your mind, body, and life.

Here's an example. *Adventure* is a core Essence of mine which I've named Skiing Black Diamonds (any adventure or challenge for me). I could ski a black diamond ski run every day to honor and feel the energy of my Essence, but that certainly isn't practical. Instead, what I look for are ways to infuse *Skiing Black Diamond* energy into my day-to-day life.

When my son was one month old, I remember that going for a walk around the block with all three of my kids, all by myself, felt just as adventurous and challenging as when I was actually going down a black diamond advanced ski run. Today I might drive home from the grocery store a new way (without even looking at my GPS), head to the beach unexpectedly with my kids, or go to the Japanese market (where I can't read or understand a word) and pick up something new to try off the shelf.

Here is Anna's story. She was an individual coaching client who realized that living into and honoring her Essences in the tiniest of ways could have a mammoth impact on her self-esteem, energy, and life.

Anna's Story

Anna, a designer and mom of two daughters who lives in Washington, DC, realized how a seemingly small, innocuous event in her daily life could honor all of her Essences.

Here is a list of Anna's top Essences.

1. Adventure
2. Love
3. Spirit
4. Connection
5. Gratitude
6. Commitment
7. Giving

One day, a fellow mom approached Anna and asked if Anna could take her two oldest children to school one morning the following week. This mom needed to take her youngest child to the doctor to have a simple procedure done.

Anna, before coaching, had been hesitant to assist fellow moms in ways requiring serious responsibility (like driving another child). The pressure and responsibility terrified her. When her friend approached her, she felt herself going into her normal "hesitate and retreat" mode. Then she remembered her Essences – who she is at her core – and the parts of her that she loved and wanted to honor even more. She decided to do something different and took the leap. She said, "Yes!" to herself and to her friend in need.

Anna tapped into all of her Essences by agreeing to take her friend's children to school that day.

- *Giving* – Giving her time and energy.
- *Commitment* – Making a promise to her friend.

- *Gratitude & Connection* – Feeling grateful that her friend trusted her enough to reach out for help.

- *Spirit & Love* – Recognizing there is something bigger than herself out there when she opened her heart to another.

- *Adventure* – Doing something new and stepping outside of her usual comfort zone.

Anna stated that "because I honored all my Essences, gratitude from the family came unexpectedly. Not only did it come in the form of a verbal thank you, but through a gift card placed in my daughter's back pack. The biggest gift, however, was that I felt that I had truly done something to change someone's life 'unexpectedly' for the better. I felt complete."

By stretching herself in this way and honoring her Essences, Anna continued to build a deep sense of potency and trust in herself which allows her to live a vivid and extraordinary life she loves.

> Imagine that you know exactly what your core Essences are. What do you believe is possible for you if you honor and live fully into them each and every day?

No One Is Honoring My Essences!

Once you uncover your top Essences, it may feel like others don't honor, agree with, or recognize your Essences. Here's the rub. It is **solely** up to you to honor your Essences. If it feels as if others aren't honoring your Essences, then it is likely time for you to make some different choices in your life.

You make choices every single minute of every single hour of your life. You choose who you spend your time with, what activities you experience, where you work, where you live, what you wear, eat, say, and think, etc. So, if you think someone isn't honoring your Essences, know that you can't change him or her, but you can make a new and different choice and change YOU.

Debby's Story

Debby, a loving and family-focused mom of three, has a strong Essence around Family Connections. She is the one who plans events for her extended family, and she feels like the glue that holds everyone together. She felt worn out and tired by this HUGE burden which fell solely on her. She wondered why no one else in her family was honoring her Essence of Family Connections. She felt resentful.

After discussing Essences on one of our Vivid Living Group calls, Debby realized she had been blaming others for not caring the way she did about creating connections among family members. She blamed others for not having the same core Essence (or at least for not acting on it the same way she did).

No matter how hard you try or how much you'd like to, you cannot change anyone else. The only person you can change is yourself. Debby doesn't know what core Essences other family members have. What Debby does know is that their actions demonstrate they are perfectly happy letting her orchestrate the family gatherings. So, using that knowledge, Debby has options.

She can choose to keep doing what she's doing, stop doing what she's doing, or find another perspective to hold as she honors her Family Connection Essence. She may choose to ask for more support from others, knowing she may or may not get it. Or she may just plan events that feel fulfilling to her. Maybe she'll only plan one gathering a year instead of the four that she traditionally planned. There are many options for her to explore. All of them focus on what is within her power to change.

Most important is that Debby makes a choice that she can live with, owns her actions as HER choice, and releases expectations that anyone else must honor her Essence. When she honors her Essence in a way that feels right and true, she may very well inspire others to do the same.

> What is something for which you blame others in your life? Change your language to own it. Once you own it, then you can choose to make a different choice, if you wish. Example: **Blame:** *"They expect me to plan and do it all and never help."* **Own it:** *"I've been choosing to do it all alone." Now, you can keep choosing to do it all alone, get creative about asking for help, or you can even decide to not do it anymore. There are endless possibilities. Get creative and think outside the box.*

To Be or Not To Be…ME!

Once you are clear about your Essences and you have practiced living into them, they can guide you to be just the person you want to be. You can increasingly show up in the world with your kids, family, friends, and colleagues in alignment with your heart, core and truth. And, your Essences can help you to make tough (or even simple) decisions in your life.

Lynne's Story

Lynne, a cosmopolitan mom of two living in Washington, DC, learned how her Essences could help her to show up more powerfully and fully with her fellow students in graduate school. She sat in a class where the discussion had turned to how to find jobs after graduation. Lynne, having had a previous career as a documentary filmmaker, knew very well what was involved in finding new jobs. She was used to regularly looking for new projects as it was a natural part of her work in the world of film. At the same time, deep down, she also had anxiety about the upcoming job search.

Near the end of the conversation she spoke up. Her back arched; she leaned way back in her chair and held her head high. She then shared her perspective about the absolute BEST practices to get a new job. A few classmates met her comments with strong resistance.

Lynne told me that instead of feeling like her spunky, open, and warm self when she spoke up in class, she felt stiff, rigid, and cold. When she looked over her Essence list she realized she had behaved exactly the opposite of her Essence of Warmth. She defines her Essence of Warmth as – open/welcoming/ generous/putting people at ease – and her posture is "leaning forward with her eyes wide open and feeling very present in her body." Warmth was nowhere to be found when she'd spoken to her classmates in that moment, and she didn't like how she felt as a result.

During our coaching call she practiced delivering her same message in a new and different way – with lots of Warmth and fully honoring her desire to share her wisdom and experience. She honored herself at her core and spoke her truth instead of acting from her fears, defenses, and old patterns.

After our call, she felt excited and hopeful. Revisiting her Essences helped Lynne become acutely aware of when she was or was not showing up in alignment with who she is and what is most important to her at her core. Then, practicing living into them helped her to know exactly what it felt like in her body and life when she lived from her heart and truth and when she didn't. Lynne now has her Essences at her fingertips to use as a tool to help her anchor into her truth and who she is at her core anytime she desires.

You, too, can use your Essences to show up in the world in the way you most desire. Uncover them. Become familiar with them. Practice living into them. Be curious about them. Keep them front and center. Eventually, you'll know when you are living a vivid and extraordinary life you love and when you are veering off your path.

When you know you took a wrong turn, simply come back to your Essences. Ask yourself which ones you were honoring, which ones you weren't, and how you can honor them next time.

In the same vein, when you are faced with decisions to make and are unsure which path to take, head in the direction that leads you toward your Essences. They are a guiding light of wisdom.

> Think of a time when you said or did something that left you feeling "off," awful, or like you didn't even recognize yourself. What part of yourself (or what Essence of yours) did you ignore in that moment?

The Essence Discovery Process

The Journal and Action Exercises at the end of this session will guide you to discover your Essences. Know that the Essence Discovery Process may take some time and conscious effort. You'll find tips for quick Essence access, and I'll walk you through the steps to dig deep to uncover them organically, if you wish.

See what you uncover at first. Then, sit with your Essences. Try them on. Keep asking yourself if all aspects of YOU are represented in the Essences you have chosen. If not, try to name what's missing and add that to your Essence list.

You don't have to find the perfect words here. If you get lost or feel overwhelmed then just go with what pops into your head first and know that you can refine things down the road. Use your body as a guide. Your body doesn't lie and it will light up when you have found a core Essence.

Emily's Story

Emily, a mom of two boys, had uncovered most of her Essences with support from her Vivid Living Coaching Group. When she reviewed her list, however, she felt that something was missing. She listened to the recording of a group call ("Get Those Ogres" coaching group call) she couldn't attend and, after listening, she shared a new understanding of the power of revisiting and revising her Essence work. She found her lost Essence.

"I missed having our session today. I waited in line for many hours to get the H1N1 flu shot for the kids only to have my car towed. Definitely had to do some breathing today...

I have to say I was reluctant to sit down this evening after a long day to listen to the recording of the call I had missed. I assumed it would not have the same impact as being on the call, but I was completely WRONG! I was engaged, I cried, AND I completed my list of Essences (thank you). Going in I had six, but I knew I was missing something. Here they are:

> *Comfort*
>
> *Empathy*
>
> *Fairness*
>
> *Openness*
>
> *Preparedness*
>
> *Resolve*
>
> *And… CONNECTIONS!!!*
>
> *(It was like a light came on and I felt complete.)*

I am in the process of naming and embodying my Essences and look forward to talking next week about Life Purpose."

Uncovering your Essences may take a mere minute. Or, you may find that it takes you hours or even days of revising and revisiting your list. Either way, trust your process and trust that you will know when you've uncovered your full list of Essences. You'll feel it in your body and you'll know it in your mind. Start with what comes easily. The rest will flow over time. Don't give up.

What is something in your life that took time, focus, and effort to complete and was totally worth it in the end? What did you learn from the process and experience along the way?

How to Know When You've Found an Essence

Just as Emily described in the example above, when you do finally uncover a true Essence it might feel like "a light came on." Other clients describe feeling solidness, tingling, warmth, ease, lightness, or heart-swelling in their bodies; some even find their eyes filling with tears when they finally uncover a sure fit.

Look for the Essences that give you a similar feeling as when you imagined feeling excited and alive during the Journal and Action Exercises from "Listen to Your BodyTruth", session III. Your body knows and will help you to recognize that you've landed on an Essence.

If you experience tightness, heaviness, stagnation, or darkness when you think of a particular Essence, there's a good chance that a "should" or old fear is lurking nearby. Let go of that Essence and look for other ones that are should-free and fear-free.

You may look at the list of Essences you collected or at the Essence Quick Pick List at the end of this session, and question the ones that stand out most to you. Maybe they seem too good to be true. Go ahead and pick them anyway. Sometimes your Ogres (all of those unhelpful and limiting thoughts and beliefs – more on them in session VI, "Get Those Ogres") pop up here and want to steal away your energy, aliveness, and greatness. Move any doubts and second-guessing aside and pick Essences that stand out or feel important to you anyway. Keep coming back to your body to help you identify your Essences. Your body knows.

> What sensations do you experience in your body when you know you are absolutely onto something true and right for you?

MORE ESSENCE EXAMPLES

Julie's Essences

I gave each Essence a unique, personal name to help it come alive for me (Journal Exercise 5).

1. ***Driving Naked*** – Freedom / Breeze On Skin / Sensations / There is Something Bigger Than Myself

2. ***Skiing Black Diamonds*** – Learning / Challenging and Believing In Myself / Growing / Push To the Edge / Believe and Do

3. ***Love Smiles*** – Open Heart / Looking / Seeing / Smiling / Ready to Give / Love / Space / Breath

4. ***Coach – Leader*** / Creating and Holding Space / Holding Others and Things BIG / Trust / Resourceful / Leading By Example / Encourage

5. ***Patty Cake*** – Fun / Use Body to Play / Be Silly and Laugh Lovingly / Games / Creative / Youthful / Energetic

6. ***Life*** – Nature / Mountains / Trees / Desert / Blue Sky / Flowers / Color / Expansive / Life Force / Ageless Wisdom / Fresh

7. ***Belly Dancer*** – Body / Freedom of Movement / Health / Flexibility / Strength / Trust in Body / Intuition

8. ***Mother Earth*** (Pachamama) – Fullness / Unending Love / Passion / Commitment / Rootedness / Stable / Wise / Warmth / Femininity / Deep Trust

Carenna's Essences

She gave each Essence a physical stance or posture to embody her Essences (Journal Exercise 6).

1. **Comfort** – Health / Feeling Strong in My Body / Beautiful Environment / Comfy Bed / Breathing Deeply

   Posture: Lying on my side resting

2. **Peace** – Rest / Deep Knowing / No Judgment / Support

   Posture: Singing

3. **Abundance** – Freedom / Beauty / Elegance / Grace / Extra Time and Money / Fun

   Posture: Laughing and Leaping

4. **Family and Friends** – Love / Caring / Understanding / Honesty From the Heart / Open Communication / Camaraderie / Sharing

   Posture: Smiles and Hugs

5. **Joy** – Fun / Silly / Carefree / Pure / Social / Games

   Posture: Spinning Around

6. **Learning** – Expanding My Mind / Knowledgeable About the World – Past, Present, and Future / Worldly

   Posture: Yoga Chair Pose – Feet Together, Knees Bent, Arms Straight Up By Ears, Torso Learning Slightly Forward

Get To Your Core

SESSION HIGHLIGHTS

- Essences are who you are, uniquely and intrinsically, at your core — the things that without, you just wouldn't be you.

- Essences are **not** values.

- Once you uncover and define your core Essences, your homework will be to practice honoring and living into them as often as possible. As you live into your Essences more and more, you will automatically find yourself living a life that feels aligned, fun, and exciting. Your confidence will soar. You'll feel more balanced and excited to wake up in the morning. You'll have absolute clarity about what is most important to you.

- Know that the process of uncovering your Essences takes some time and maybe even a few different revisions.

- Use your body to help you find your Essences. Your body doesn't lie, and it will know when you've uncovered a core Essence.

- It is solely up to you to honor your Essences. You can't change others, but you surely can make some different choices for yourself.

- Your Essences guide you to be just the person you want to be in the world. They help you to show up fully in the world with your kids, family, friends, and colleagues. They ensure you are aligned with your heart, core, and inner truth.

It's time to uncover your unique Essences. The "Get to Your Core" Journal and Action Exercises will guide you to know unquestionably who you are at your core and what is most important to you. This tool is super powerful (and fun!). Enjoy!

Get to Your Core

JOURNAL EXERCISES

* *Reminder: No need to do all the exercises. Focus on the one/s that excite or interest you the most.*

The Essence Discovery Process

Enjoy the rich Essence Discovery Process and steps below.

If you feel stuck or are short on time, then head over to the Essence Quick Pick List on page 134 to jumpstart your Essence Discovery Process.

1. **Explore Peak Experiences**. A great place to begin to identify your Essences is to revisit your Peak Experiences. Identify at least two special moments when you felt the most alive or "on fire." These are times when you felt the most YOU, and felt energized and super excited about life, even if it was only for second. List the words that describe your experience. This list is the beginning of your Essence list. You'll narrow the list down later on. For now, see how many words you can collect. If you need help finding the words to describe your Peak Experiences then use the Essence Quick Pick List on page 134.

    *Example: **Peak Experience:** When Mark plays on stage with his band.*

    1. *Ecstatic*
    2. *Alive*
    3. *Going All Out*

    4. *Trust*

    5. *Present*

    6. *Spiritual*

    7. *Connection*

    8. *True to Myself*

A Peak Experience _____

    1.

    2.

    3.

    4.

    5.

    6.

    7.

    8.

    9.

    10.

A Peak Experience _____

    1.

    2.

    3.

4.

5.

6.

7.

8.

9.

10.

2. **What irks you?** Another way to identify your Essences is to name what really upsets you and then find its opposite. Every moment of annoyance in your life is a likely cue that a specific Essence is not being honored.

Name the annoyance. Then flip it over and name the exact opposite – the opposite may very well be an Essence of yours. Add the words you collect in the Opposite of What Irks You column, to your Essence list. You'll narrow the list down in the next step.

Example: Francine can't stand feeling stuck or caged in. When she flipped feeling stuck or caged in 180 degrees (named the opposite) she discovered two Essences of hers – freedom and autonomy.

What Irks You	**Opposite of What Irks You**
Example: Feeling Stuck or Caged In	*Freedom & Autonomy*

1.

2.

3.

4.

3. **Choose your top five to seven Essences.** What top five to seven Essences are uniquely you, that without, you just wouldn't be YOU?

   a. Take the list of Essence words that you collected from going through the two exercises above or take your list of starred words from the Essence Quick Pick List on page 134 and narrow the list down.

   b. Keep words on the list that feel like a sure fit. Cut the list in half, again and again, until you are left with your top five to seven Essences. It might seem like there are a lot of words that speak to you. Trust that as you go through this process you will narrow the list to your top five to seven Essences.

   Remember to look to your body as a guide. When an Essence is a sure fit, you may notice a solidness, ease, tingling, aliveness, heart-swelling, tears, or fullness in your chest, stomach, shoulders, or head. Find the Essences that give you a similar feeling to when you imagined feeling excited and alive during the exercises from the Listen to Your BodyTruth section, session III, on pages 92-102. Remember your body knows and doesn't lie.

   c. Trust that as you go through this process you'll pick the words that are right for you. It's OK to let some words go even if you feel connected to them. You may find that you bring them back later to help you define your top Essences.

Top Essences List

1.

2.

3.

4.

5.

6.

7.

For exercises 3 - 7, you may find the **Essence Matrix** on page 136 helpful to track your brainstorming and capture your results.

> You can also download a copy of the **Essence Matrix** at www.vividliving.net/freebookdownloads

4. **Define your Essences.** What do your Essences mean to you? Use a string of adjectives or short phrases to describe your unique definition of each Essence. Very often, Essences that didn't quite make it to the top of your Essence list are found in the string of descriptions. See where you can consolidate. When you are done, ask yourself if all of you is represented here. If not, then add in the missing Essences and define them.

   Example: **Challenge** = *something new / adventure / push to my edge / believe and do / trust*

   1. (Your Essence) = _____ / _____ / _____ / _____ / _____

   2.

3.

4.

5.

6.

7.

5. **Name your Essences**. Find a unique name that embodies the energy of each Essence. You might choose a metaphor, or a name based on a song, book, picture, movie or time when you most embodied that specific Essence. Naming the Essence in this unique way gives the Essence more aliveness and depth which brings it deeper into your body. Create a name that fits for you.

   Example: **Challenge** = *Skiing Black Diamonds*

   1.

   2.

   3.

   4.

   5.

   6.

   7.

6. **Embody your Essences**. What is a movement, posture, or yoga pose (if you are familiar with yoga) that embodies the energy of your Essence? Use the pose and any physical representations to keep your Essence close and alive.

Example: **Skiing Black Diamonds** = *Standing as if I'm holding ski poles, knees bent, weight forward, ready to head down the mountain. I'm going for it.*

1.
2.
3.
4.
5.
6.
7.

7. **Rate it**. How much are you currently living into each of your Essences? (0 = Not at All, 10 = All the Time)

1.
2.
3.
4.
5.
6.
7.

Essence Quick Pick List
If you feel stuck or are short on time, then use the Essence Quick Pick List on pages 134-135 to jumpstart your Essence Discovery Process.

1. Go through this list and put a star by every word that describes who you are at your core. It's OK to put a star by many words!

2. Next, review the starred words and cut your list in half, over and over, until you are left with your top five to seven Essences. Keep the words on your list that feel like a sure fit.

   Remember to look to your body as a guide. When an Essence is a sure fit, you may notice a solidness, ease, tingling, aliveness, heart-swelling, tears, or fullness in your chest, stomach, shoulders, or head. Find the Essences that give you a similar feeling to when you imagined feeling excited and alive during the exercises from "Listen to Your BodyTruth," session III, on pages 92-102. Your body knows and doesn't lie.

3. Trust that as you go through this process you'll pick the words that are right for you. It's OK to let some words go even if you feel connected to them. You may find that you bring them back later to help you define your top Essences.

4. Now I'll walk you through the rest of the Essence Discovery Process beginning with Journal Exercise 4. Here you'll get to see other Essence examples along the way. Feel free to use the Essence Matrix provided on page 136 (or download it at www.vividliving.net/freebookdownloads) to help you track your brainstorming and capture your Essence results, if you wish.

5. If it's really hard to pull your Essences off the Essence Quick Pick List, then go to Journal Exercise 1 – Explore Peak Experiences, and Journal Exercise 2 – What Irks You?, to create a list of possible Essences for yourself.

Essence Matrix: Create Your Essence List

Use the Essence Matrix on page 136 to track your brainstorming and to help you define and bring to life your top core Essences. Further details are outlined in Journal Exercises 3 - 7 above.

> Visit www.vividliving.net/freebookdownloads to download a blank copy of this **Essence Matrix** for you to use on your Essence Discovery journey.

ESSENCE QUICK PICK LIST

#	Essence	#	Essence	#	Essence
1.	Abundance	43.	Connection	85.	Exhilaration
2.	Accessibility	44.	Consciousness	86.	Experience
3.	Accomplishment	45.	Consistency	87.	Exploration
4.	Accuracy	46.	Contentment	88.	Expressiveness
5.	Acknowledgement	47.	Contribution	89.	Exuberance
6.	Activeness	48.	Conviction	90.	Fairness
7.	Adoration	49.	Conviviality	91.	Faith
8.	Adventure	50.	Cooperation	92.	Family
9.	Affection	51.	Courage	93.	Fascination
10.	Aggressiveness	52.	Courtesy	94.	Fearlessness
11.	Agility	53.	Craftiness	95.	Fitness
12.	Alertness	54.	Creativity	96.	Flexibility
13.	Ambition	55.	Credibility	97.	Flow
14.	Appreciation	56.	Curiosity	98.	Focus
15.	Approachability	57.	Daring	99.	Fortitude
16.	Assertiveness	58.	Decisiveness	100.	Freedom
17.	Attentiveness	59.	Delight	101.	Friendliness
18.	Availability	60.	Depth	102.	Fun
19.	Awareness	61.	Determination	103.	Gallantry
20.	Awe	62.	Devotion	104.	Generosity
21.	Balance	63.	Diligence	105.	Giving
22.	Beauty	64.	Direction		
23.	Bliss	65.	Directness		
24.	Boldness	66.	Discovery		
25.	Bravery	67.	Diversity		
26.	Calmness	68.	Dreaming		
27.	Camaraderie	69.	Drive		
28.	Capability	70.	Dynamism		
29.	Care	71.	Eagerness		
30.	Challenge	72.	Ecstasy		
31.	Charity	73.	Education		
32.	Cheerfulness	74.	Effectiveness		
33.	Clarity	75.	Efficiency		
34.	Cleanliness	76.	Elation		
35.	Clear-mindedness	77.	Elegance		
36.	Closeness	78.	Empathy		
37.	Comfort	79.	Encouragement		
38.	Commitment	80.	Endurance		
39.	Compassion	81.	Energy		
40.	Composure	82.	Enjoyment		
41.	Confidence	83.	Enthusiasm		
42.	Congruency	84.	Excitement		

Get to Your Core – Session IV

106. Grace	128. Inspiration	149. Openness	171. Relaxation	193. Spirit
107. Gratitude	129. Integrity	150. Optimism	172. Resilience	194. Spontaneity
108. Gregariousness	130. Intelligence	151. Originality	173. Resolve	195. Synergy
109. Growth	131. Intensity	152. Outrageousness	174. Resourcefulness	196. Teamwork
110. Guidance	132. Intimacy	153. Passion	175. Respect	197. Thankfulness
111. Harmony	133. Intuition	154. Peace	176. Rest	198. Thoughtfulness
112. Health	134. Inventiveness	155. Perkiness	177. Richness	199. Tranquility
113. Heart	135. Joy	156. Perseverance	178. Rigor	200. Trust
114. Helpfulness	136. Justice	157. Persistence	179. Sacredness	201. Truth
115. Heroism	137. Kindness	158. Persuasiveness	180. Saintliness	202. Usefulness
116. Holiness	138. Leadership	159. Playfulness	181. Selflessness	203. Variety
117. Honesty	139. Learning	160. Pleasure	182. Self-reliance	204. Vigor
118. Honor	140. Liberty	161. Potency	183. Sensuality	205. Vision
119. Hopefulness	141. Liveliness	162. Precision	184. Serenity	206. Vitality
120. Humility	142. Love	163. Preparedness	185. Sexuality	207. Vivacity
121. Humor	143. Loyalty	164. Proactivity	186. Sharing	208. Warmth
122. Imagination	144. Making a difference	165. Purity	187. Silence	209. Wisdom
123. Impact	145. Mellowness	166. Reason	188. Silliness	210. Wonder
124. Independence	146. Mindfulness	167. Reasonableness	189. Simplicity	211. Youthfulness
125. Ingenuity	147. Mysteriousness	168. Recognition	190. Sincerity	212. Zeal
126. Inquisitiveness	148. Open-mindedness	169. Recreation	191. Skillfulness	
127. Insightfulness		170. Reflection	192. Solitude	

ESSENCE MATRIX

CHOOSE YOUR ESSENCE	DEFINE YOUR ESSENCE	NAME YOUR ESSENCE	EMBODY YOUR ESSENCE	RATE IT!
List your top five to seven Essences – who you are uniquely and intrinsically at your core – the things that make you the real YOU!	Develop a string of adjectives or short phrases to describe your unique definition of each Essence.	Capture a name that embodies the energy of each Essence. Maybe a metaphor, or a name based on a song, book, picture, movie or time when you most embodied that Essence.	Select a moment, posture, or yoga pose (if you are familiar with yoga) that embodies the energy of your Essence.	Rate how much you are currently living into each of your Essences. (0 = Not at All, 10 = All the Time)
1.				
2.				
3.				
4.				
5.				
6.				
7.				

Get to Your Core

ACTION EXERCISES

* *Reminder: No need to do all the exercises. Focus on the one/s that excite or interest you the most.*

1. **Bring your Essences into your cells.** Write or print your Essences on 10 sticky notes and post them up everywhere. Post them in every prominent place that you can – on your bathroom mirror, refrigerator (in your veggie drawer), TV, bedpost, dashboard, computer screen, desk, or in a closet. This will remind you of who you are every minute. It takes reminders and practice to transformation your life into an extraordinary and vivid life you love. Remind and surprise yourself. For more ideas and ways to remind yourself of your Essences check out the Suggested Structures List on page 24.

2. **Live into your Essences daily.** Find a way, big or little, to live into your Essences. Do this every day for each Essence or choose one or two Essences to focus on daily.

    Here is my list of my Essences and how I lived into every single one of them in a day.

    - *Driving Naked* – I went for a walk and stood in a spot on a hill by my house and saw the ocean on one side and the mountains on the other. I raised out my arms and took in five delicious deep breaths.

    - *Skiing Black Diamonds* – I took all three kids to Costco by myself.

    - *Love Smiles* – While at Costco I smiled warmly at a complete stranger.

- **Coach** – I acknowledged my friend for her strength and wisdom when she calmly confronted a co-worker.
- **Patty Cake** – I played tickles with my kids.
- **Life** – I breathed in and appreciated the green grass in my backyard.
- **Belly Dancer** – I appreciated and thanked my strong legs, hips and belly as I walked up a hill.
- **Mother Earth** (Pachamama) – I hugged my children and sent them love through my arms and heart.

> Want to hear clients describe their Essences and how they use them to live a vivid and extraordinary life they love? Then visit www.vividliving.net/freebookdownloads to hear the client **Essence Stories Audio Recordings.**

3. **Do the movement/posture/pose for each Essence.** Hold an Essence movement, posture or pose for one minute. Breathe and visualize yourself living into and feeling the energy of your Essence. Do this every day for each Essence of yours or choose one or two Essences to focus on daily.

4. **Pick and choose.** Every morning or evening imagine what the upcoming day holds for you. Ask yourself what Essences you want to focus on for that day to help you live as you most desire. Next, imagine living into them as you go through your day. Be who you most want to be, even if just in your mind's eye. Your body will follow.

One day I was being interviewed by Sheri Kaye Hoff for her Interviews with the Experts Series, about my work as a Life Coach. When I woke up in the morning I was excited and nervous. I knew that I could use an extra dose of my Coach, Skiing Black Diamonds, and Love Smiles Essence energy that day. I reminded myself about them all morning and then, right before the call, took on my skiing down the mountain pose, smiled lots of big love smiles, and sat in my backyard where I usually coach to infuse them into my body fully before the interview. Infusing my life and body with my Essence energy that morning helped to keep me calm, grounded, and true to myself. I showed up fully. I had a ball.

5. **Notice and practice.** Notice when you make decisions consistent with your Essences and when you take a divergent path. What do you experience in your body or say to yourself when you follow each path? Choose to head in the direction that leads you to honor your Essences. It is all about choice and practice.

What's My Homework?

GET TO YOUR CORE SESSION IV

What actions or reflections are you committed to do, to practice, or to think about? Let these be things that interest, excite or even terrify you. Challenge yourself!

1.

2.

3.

4.

Create structures. Do you think it might be challenging for you to remember to do your homework or keep your commitments? If so, then pick out some structures to put in place to remind you of them. It's easy to get excited about your commitments and intentions. The hard part is keeping them. Structures can help.

> Look at page 24 to see the **Suggested Structures List**. Or, visit www.vividliving.net/freebookdownloads to download the **Suggested Structures List.**

Vivid Living Resources

SESSION IV

FREE Digital Downloads

⬇ **Essence Stories Audio Recording**. Download and listen as clients share how they put their Essences to use daily to live vivid and extraordinary lives.

www.vividliving.net/freebookdownloads

⬇ **Essence Matrix**. Download a blank copy of the Essence Matrix to use on your Essence Discovery journey. It can help you to define your top five to seven core Essences. Download it and make it your own.

www.vividliving.net/freebookdownloads

Vivid Living Check-In

SESSION IV

1. What have I learned?

2. What challenges did I run into?

3. What do I want to remember that will help me to live a vivid and extraordinary life I love?

4. Fill in a Vivid Living Thermometer today. See what's shifting for you as you journey along your Vivid Living adventure.

VIVID LIVING THERMOMETER   Date _____

AREA OF YOUR LIFE	RATING 0-10
CAREER	
ENVIRONMENT	
FAMILY	
FRIENDS	
FUN	
HEALTH	
ME AS MOM	
MONEY	
PERSONAL GROWTH	
SIGNIFICANT OTHER	
SPIRITUALITY	
OVERALL VIVID LIVING	

AREA OF FOCUS _____
COMMITMENT _____
_____

Notes

Your Life Purpose

SESSION V

Strong lives are motivated by dynamic purposes.
Kenneth Hildebrand

Find a purpose in life so big it will challenge every capacity to be at your best.
David McKay

We all have the extraordinary coded within us waiting to be released.
Jean Houston

Are you starting to see how these tools – The Vivid Living Thermometer, listening to your BodyTalk and using your Essences – can help you to live your life with more ease, less guilt, more confidence, and increased balance? Here is one more tool to anchor you into your truth and passion. During this session the focus is on your Life Purpose – the Unique Impact that you are meant to have on this world. Sounds powerful, doesn't it? Wait until you live it day in and day out, minute to minute… The world is waiting for YOU!

Your Life Purpose

What is your Life Purpose? Each of us has a unique purpose – every single one of us. For some, your Life Purpose is clear. Others have to search a bit more. I'm not just talking about knowing who your partner will be, how many kids you might have, or what your profession or hobbies will be.

Don't get me wrong. These things are important and play a big role in defining who you are. However, when I talk about Life Purpose, I'm talking about your Big Intention and the Unique Impact you have on the world around you. Your true purpose gives your life meaning and direction. By the time you complete this session you'll have all the tools you need to uncover your Life Purpose.

Sam's Story

Sam, an amazingly intuitive, spunky woman was getting a divorce and knew this time in her life was a chance for her to reinvent herself from the inside out. She knew the way she had been living her life wasn't working. She was ready to dive deep, uncover her truth, and live it, unabashedly, for the first time. She signed on for some individual life coaching with me.

One of the first things she did was uncover her Life Purpose Statement. Here it is:

"My Life Purpose is to use my intelligence and creativity to make a difference and create a world that is better than when I found it."

Sam's personal life was clearly shifting. She also wanted to make major changes in her professional life. The path here was dimly lit and felt hard for her to identify.

Sam entertained the idea of becoming a consultant in her previous field of OD (Organization Development) as a way to make some money before following her true passion. When she thought about consulting, however, she noticed heaviness and pressure in her heart and body. It quickly became clear that this decision did not honor her Life Purpose. Once she committed to only doing work in line with her Life Purpose things began to flow.

Sam realized she could choose to do consulting work in OD that supported her to use her *"intelligence and creativity to make a difference and create a world that is better than when [I] found it."* She discovered the freedom to say, *"No!"* to projects that weren't aligned with her Life Purpose.

This realization freed up energy and space in her life. Sam found herself rekindling a writing project hiding under the professional surface of her life for years. She let it out and, after just a few short weeks of coaching, made huge strides toward seeing her passion project through to fruition – a project that, potentially, could change her professional trajectory.

Sam learned firsthand and very quickly how powerful she can be and how easily things can flow when she follows her Life Purpose. She now keeps her Life Purpose Statement front and center as a daily reminder of her Big Intention and the Unique Impact she is meant to have in this world. It drives her, feeds her, and guides her.

> What's possible for you when you live purposefully and powerfully in your life?

Discover Your Life Purpose

In the Journal Exercises section at the end of this session you will find the steps to follow to support you to create your Life Purpose Statement. Here is a template you can use and examples of others' Life Purpose Statements to get your creative juices flowing.

Life Purpose Statement Template
(Adapted with permission from CTI.)

I am the _____ (*who I'm being*) **that** _____ (*the impact I'm having*).

Life Purpose Statement Examples

- *I am the rock in your shoe that reminds you to live deliberately.*

- *I am the sun that melts the ice so you can dig deep, grow, and flourish.*

- *I am the confetti that makes the party of life colorful.*

- *My love warms the way for others to fearlessly live their truth and passion.*

- *I create community that makes life fulfilling, colorful, and fun.*

You'll get information about your Life Purpose from exploring any of the Journal Exercises at the end of this session. If creating an actual statement, like the ones above, doesn't excite you, then skip it and find other exercises in the Journal Exercises section that do excite you.

> Why bother living into your Life Purpose?

Your Body Knows Your Life Purpose

Keep looking for cues from your body as you explore your Life Purpose. You'll know you're onto something when you feel excited, lit up, energized, and/or alive in your body. If you feel pressure, tension, heaviness, or "stuckness" when you think about or try on your Life Purpose, then check to see if you adopted a Life Purpose you think (or someone else thinks) you **should** live instead of one that is truly yours at your core.

Know that when you do strike gold and find your true Life Purpose it may very well bring tears to your eyes. Often, when you bring yourself to tears it is because you tapped into your absolute truth. And, if you don't tear up so easily then look for smiles or feeling moved, excited, or lit up.

If you have any of these experiences, there is a good chance you are on your way to uncovering your Life Purpose.

> Imagine opening your heart – fully – to your Life Purpose.
> What's possible for you from this place?

Live on Purpose

Once you uncover your unique Life Purpose, remind yourself of it constantly so you can tap into its energy whenever you want a pick-me-up, some direction, or inspiration. I guarantee that if you put it in a drawer or on a shelf and never think about it, it won't mean much to you or be very useful.

If, however, you use it, keep it top of mind and practice living it, then, with time, you will naturally live your Life Purpose. You will use it as a guide without much conscious thought or energy. You will be closer than ever to living your vivid and extraordinary life. When you live into and honor your Life Purpose fully, there's no space for fear.

Let's say you're committed to reminding yourself of your Life Purpose. Now what? The next step is to live into it. Find big and small ways to live into your Life Purpose every day. It can guide all you do and how you live your life. It can steer your interactions, influence big and small decisions, and guide where you put your energy and attention.

Julie's Life Purpose Statement

This is my Life Purpose Statement.

> *I am the spark that ignites the fire of belief in you that you can live a vivid and extraordinary life you love.*

Here are some examples of ways I live into my Life Purpose daily.

- I acknowledge how loving my daughter is when she gives her little brother a big hug: she's living lovingly and unabashedly.

- I start a new Vivid Living Group or work on a session in this book – to ignite the flame in others to clearly follow their path toward Vivid Living.

- When I notice I'm feeling down or uncertain, I take a breath and imagine myself having the impact I most desire on the people around me and in the world. I reconnect to this feeling and image until it infuses my body and life with renewed energy and focus and allows the uncertainty to drop away.

> What would your life be like if your Life Purpose drove everything you did, said, and thought?

Be Bold

Once you know what your Life Purpose is, you can use it to guide your decisions and interactions. Below is an example of how a client used her Life Purpose Statement to show up courageously and with more clarity than ever before at an important work meeting.

Andrea's Story

Andrea, a fun and spunky writer and executive in the entertainment business, shared with her Vivid Living Coaching Group just how helpful living into her Life Purpose Statement was when she met with the president of her organization. Here's what she shared.

"I ended up doing a formal presentation for the president of the network last week and it was one of the most difficult weeks of my life. I had a lot of tools to reach for, one of which was calling my mom to cry and let it out. That is a good tool. But a brand new one was asking myself how to be true to

my life's purpose during this challenge: 'I am the giggle that erupts in a room bringing others together.' How do you do that while presenting to one of the most powerful people in Hollywood? Well, it did exactly what it needed to. It cancelled out 'corporate Andrea,' the persona I am not comfortable with, and as soon as I gave myself permission to do that and be myself (and prepared and rehearsed like crazy) I actually killed it. My boss and his boss were thrilled, as was my team (there were about 30+ people in the room).

I'm still marveling at how I did it. I was terrified. And then, of course, I'm preparing to make some drastic life changes that are even scarier. But I know in my body they are the right choices for me."

As Andrea discovered, honoring and living into your Life Purpose can give you the clarity, direction, and even the freedom to be the YOU you most want to be under any circumstance. Most importantly, Andrea was able to use the power of her Life Purpose Statement because she kept it front and center as a daily tool and resource.

> What does it look and feel like for you to live an exceptional life?

Your Life Purpose

SESSION HIGHLIGHTS

- Your Life Purpose is your Big Intention and the Unique Impact that YOU have on the world around you. Your Life Purpose gives your life meaning and direction.

- Once you uncover your unique Life Purpose Statement, remind yourself of it constantly so you can tap into its energy whenever you want a pick-me-up, some direction, or inspiration.

- Find big and little ways to live into your Life Purpose every day. It can be a guide in all you do and how you live your life. It can steer your interactions, help you to make big and little decisions, and guide where you put your energy and attention.

- Keep looking to your body as you uncover your Life Purpose. You'll know you're on to something when you smile, feel excited, lit up, light, energized, and/or alive. Know that when you do finally strike gold and find your true Life Purpose it may very well bring tears to your eyes or make your heart swell. Very often when we bring ourselves to tears it is because we are tapping into our absolute truth.

When you wake up each morning and live into your Life Purpose and Essences, even when things are hard and the road is bumpy or full of detours (because it gets this way at times for all of us), you will still know which road is yours and which road leads home – to Vivid Living.

Use the Journal and Action Exercises in this session to uncover your unique and powerful Life Purpose.

Your Life Purpose

JOURNAL EXERCISES

* *Reminder: No need to do all the exercises. Focus on the one/s that excite or interest you the most.*

Life Purpose

1. **Create Your Life Purpose Statement**: Use the template below to help you uncover your unique Life Purpose Statement.

    If this template doesn't work for you then feel free to use the other Journal Exercises to help you shape a Life Purpose Statement.

    I am the _____ (who I'm being) **that** _____ (the impact I'm having).
    (Template adapted with permission from CTI.)

    a. Use the Life Purpose Statement Template above to help you create your own unique Life Purpose Statement.
    b. Let your statement describe who you are **being** and the **impact** you have on others or the world. Feel free to use a metaphor. Bottom line it. Keep it clear, strong, positive and in present tense. Be silly, grandiose, or flowery – whatever moves you. Be specific and mention your impact on others. Look to your body to find words that resonate for you. You may choose to use words that described your Essences or words that show up when you do the Journal Exercises below.

    c. Close your eyes and take a few breaths. Maybe even choose a breathing exercise from the Breath Work list in session III.

    d. Open your eyes and write, write, write. Keep writing different versions of statements that have some resonance until one reverberates in your whole body. Write until you find the one that makes you smile, makes your heart swell, or maybe even brings tears to your eyes.

    e. If you get stuck, ask your fears and doubts to leave the room. Send them to the moon or put them in a box. Very often when clients get stuck it is because fears and doubts (I call these Ogres and will talk about them more in session VI, "Get Those Ogres.") are getting in the way. Move them aside and just start writing – no need to be perfect. You can keep editing and changing the words as you go. Just keep being curious. See what comes.

    f. If you get really stuck, then put down this exercise, skip to some of the other Journal Exercises, and come back later.

Life Purpose Statement Examples:

- *I am the rock in your shoe that reminds you to live deliberately.*

- *I am the sun that melts the ice so you can dig deep, grow, and flourish.*

- *I am the confetti that makes the party of life colorful.*

- *My love warms the way for others to fearlessly live their truth, and passion.*

- *I am the spark that ignites the fire of belief in you that you can live a vivid and extraordinary life you love.*

Begin writing your Life Purpose Statement here…

I am the _____
(who I'm being) that _____
_____ (the impact I'm having).

I am the _____
(who I'm being) that _____
_____ (the impact I'm having).

I am the _____
(who I'm being) that _____
_____ (the impact I'm having).

I am the _____
(who I'm being) that _____
_____ (the impact I'm having).

2. **Life Purpose Visualizations**

If you're not sure how to do a visualization then see page 21 for Visualization suggestions. Use the blank spaces provided between questions to capture your thoughts and experience.

    a. Imagine yourself at your 70th birthday thinking back on your life. What stands out most for you? Ask your 70-year-old self how you got to where he/she is from where you are today and what was most important along the way.

    b. Imagine you are standing in front of a large group of people and you have just said something that has changed them and you forever. What was it that you said and what was the impact you had on these people?

c. What do you want people to say about you when you leave the room?

d. Think about a time when you were absolutely on fire, your body tingled, you didn't care what anyone else thought of you, and you were alive (a.k.a., A Peak Experience)! Where were you? What were you doing? Who was around you? What impact did you have on them?

Life Appreciation

These inquiries can help you to get a sense of what you most appreciate in life and what is most important to you. What you uncover here may inform your Life Purpose.

1. **The Mega Gratitude List**. Write a list of 100 different things you are grateful for. *If you don't think you can come up with 100 things right this minute then start small. Write down 2 things, 5 things, or 10 things you are grateful for. You maybe be surprised at how your list starts to grow once you get going. Feel free to add to this list over time.*

The Mega Gratitude List

1.
2.
3.
4.
5.
6.
7.
8.
9.
10.
11.
12.
13.
14.
15.
16.
17.
18.
19.
20.
21.
22.
23.
24.
25.
26.
27.
28.
29.
30.
31.
32.
33.
34.
35.
36.
37.
38.
39.
40.
41.
42.
43.
44.
45.
46.
47.
48.
49.
50.
51.
52.
53.
54.
55.
56.
57.
58.
59.
60.
61.
62.
63.
64.
65.
66.
67.
68.
69.
70.
71.
72.
73.
74.
75.
76.
77.
78.
79.
80.
81.
82.
83.
84.
85.
86.
87.
88.
89.
90.
91.
92.
93.
94.
95.
96.
97.
98.
99.
100.

2. **Daily Gratitude List.** Every night this week before going to bed write down at least three things that you appreciated or are thankful for about the day and/or your life.

Monday	
Tuesday	
Wednesday	
Thursday	
Friday	
Saturday	
Sunday	

3. **100 Things to Do in Your Lifetime.** Write a list of 100 things you want to do in your lifetime on the next page. This is a fun Journal Exercise to get you thinking about your short- and long-term dreams, desires, passions, and wishes.

Visit www.vividliving.net/freebookdownloads to see
Julie's 100 Things to Do in Your Lifetime List.

100 Things to Do in My Lifetime List

1.
2.
3.
4.
5.
6.
7.
8.
9.
10.
11.
12.
13.
14.
15.
16.
17.
18.
19.
20.
21.
22.
23.
24.
25.
26.
27.
28.
29.
30.
31.
32.
33.
34.
35.
36.
37.
38.
39.
40.
41.
42.
43.
44.
45.
46.
47.
48.
49.
50.
51.
52.
53.
54.
55.
56.
57.
58.
59.
60.
61.
62.
63.
64.
65.
66.
67.
68.
69.
70.
71.
72.
73.
74.
75.
76.
77.
78.
79.
80.
81.
82.
83.
84.
85.
86.
87.
88.
89.
90.
91.
92.
93.
94.
95.
96.
97.
98.
99.
100.

Your Life Purpose

ACTION EXERCISES

* *Reminder: No need to do all the exercises. Focus on the one/s that excite or interest you the most.*

1. **Live into your Life Purpose in some way, big or little, every day**. Here are some structures to help remind you of your Life Purpose. See page 24 for a list of even more Suggested Structures.

    a. **Post it up**. Write your Life Purpose on 10 sticky notes and put them up at home and/or work – anywhere you can think of. Put them in places that will surprise you like in your refrigerator or medicine cabinet, in your underwear drawer, or next to your cereal boxes.

    b. **Share it!** Share your Life Purpose with as at least three people. When you write it or say it, you get your energy moving in the direction of your Life Purpose. Sometimes it is just dang scary to commit to Vivid Living. Writing, saying, and sharing your commitments helps you to believe you can do it. Go for it!

    c. **Live it.** How many different ways (big or tiny) can you find to live into and honor your Life Purpose in one day? Challenge yourself.

2. **Create a Life Purpose business card**. Sometimes when clients decide to make the shift from work to family to be home with their kids (or even when they are in the process of switching jobs), they feel title-less and purpose-less. Creating a Life Pur-

pose business card can help you to own, in a fun and powerful way, the vivid and extraordinary life you are creating for yourself during any time of transition.

- a. **Type it**. Put your Life Purpose Statement on a business card. Add your name and contact information.

- b. **New title**. Give yourself a new title that is reflective of your Life Purpose Statement. Put it on your card.

- c. **Print it**. It is easy and inexpensive these days to print business cards. You can do it on your computer or look online to find companies that will send you free business cards.

- d. **Claim it**. Give your new business cards out to as many people as you can. Share your Life Purpose and new title with as many people as possible.

- e. **Email Signature**. An earth-friendly alternative is to add your Life Purpose Statement and new title to your email signature.

3. **Get your Life Purpose into your body.**

- a. **Choose a Life Purpose movement**. What is a movement, posture, or yoga pose (if you are familiar with yoga) that embodies the energy of your Life Purpose? Use the pose, movement, or posture to keep your Life Purpose close and alive.

- b. **Embody your Life Purpose**. While exercising, walking, or doing other movement visualize yourself living into your Essences and Life Purpose – living a vivid and extraordinary life you love. Feel it, see it, and breathe it in as you move your body. You will soak your intentions deep into your cells through active movement and visualization. Here you are using your mind and body together to help create a vivid and extraordinary life you love.

4. **Create a vision board.** A vision board is visual representation of what you want, what you are creating, and where you are heading. It is usually a fairly large piece of paper or cardboard that you decorate with words, pictures, shapes, textures, and/or colors that represent your life if there were absolutely no obstacles – living your life at a 10!

   You can use the areas from your Vivid Living Thermometer – Career, Environment, Family, Friends, Fun, Health, Me as Mom, Money, Personal Growth, Significant Other, and Spirituality – to help guide you as you create your Vivid Living Vision Board. You can also include representations of your Essences and Life Purpose. Get creative and have fun here.

   a. **Hang it up.** Hang your vision board up someplace prominent where you will see it often every single day.

   b. **Look at it.** Spend at least five minutes a day looking at your vision board (meditating on it) and/or envisioning and feeling yourself living the life represented in the Vision Board. What do you notice in your body when you imagine living that life? What smells do you smell, what sounds do you hear, what do you think and feel when you imagine living that glorious life? Dive into that world and place. It is your extraordinary life!

Your Life Purpose – Session V 163

Vision Board Example - Julie's 2010 Vision Board

What's My Homework?

YOUR LIFE PURPOSE SESSION V

What actions or reflections are you committed to do, to practice, or to think about? Let these be things that interest, excite or even terrify you. Challenge yourself!

1.

2.

3.

4.

Create structures. Do you think it might be challenging for you to remember to do your homework or keep your commitments? If so, then pick out some structures to put in place to remind you of them. It's easy to get excited about your commitments and intentions. The hard part is keeping them. Structures can help.

> Look at page 24 to see the **Suggested Structures List**. Or, visit www.vividliving.net/freebookdownloads to download the **Suggested Structures List.**

Vivid Living Resources

SESSION V

FREE Digital Downloads

12 Inspirational Life Purpose Quotes. View and download 12 of my favorite inspirational Life Purpose quotes here:

www.vividliving.net/freebookdownloads

Julie's Top 100 Things to Do in Your Lifetime List. View Julie's Top 100 Things to Do in Your Lifetime List here:

www.vividliving.net/freebookdownloads

Recommended Reading

Creating Your Best Life: The Ultimate Life List Guide by Caroline Adams Miller and Dr. Michael B. Frisch

10-10-10 by Suzy Welch

Co Active Coaching: New Skills for Coaching People Toward Success in Work and Life by Laura Whitworth, Karen Kimsey-House, Henry Kimsey-House, Phillip Sandahl

Vivid Living Check-In

SESSION V

1. What have I learned?

2. What challenges did I run into?

3. What do I want to remember that will help me to live a vivid and extraordinary life I love?

4. Fill in a Vivid Living Thermometer today. See what's shifting for you as you journey along your Vivid Living adventure.

VIVID LIVING THERMOMETER Date _____

AREA OF YOUR LIFE	RATING 0-10
CAREER	
ENVIRONMENT	
FAMILY	
FRIENDS	
FUN	
HEALTH	
ME AS MOM	
MONEY	
PERSONAL GROWTH	
SIGNIFICANT OTHER	
SPIRITUALITY	
OVERALL VIVID LIVING	

AREA OF FOCUS _____
COMMITMENT _____
_____

Notes

Get Those Ogres

SESSION VI

> *Too many folks go through life running
> from something that isn't after them.*
> **Anonymous**

> *Fear grows in darkness; if you think there's a
> bogeyman around, turn on the light.*
> **Dorothy Thompson**

> *While one person hesitates because he feels inferior,
> the other is busy making mistakes and becoming superior.*
> **Henry Link**

Here we go – session VI. You're almost there!

- You know how to use the *Vivid Living Thermometer* to give you a snapshot of how fulfilling your life is in any given moment. You can now clearly choose areas of your life to intentionally transform.

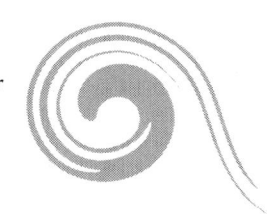

- *You know how to recognize the language of your body – your BodyTruth – which you can use along with the wisdom of your mind to make decisions and choices in line with your true self.*

- *You've uncovered your core Essences and know what it feels like when you live into them: your life starts to hum, you feel bold, and you are unstoppable.*

- *You know what your Life Purpose is. You are finding more and more ways to honor it and to live into your Big Intention and Unique Impact every single day.*

The tools above will help you to live a vivid and extraordinary life you love, for sure. And, for many of you, maybe even most of you, the information in this session will be where the really juicy and life transforming work unfolds. If it gets hard, don't give up. Hang in there… It will pay off!

This session is where you'll find all of those sneaky Ogres that hold you back from Vivid Living by sabotaging you or feeding you doses of fear and anxiety.

If you feel anxious or scared as we head into this session, that's OK – that's just an Ogre hard at work trying to make you miserable…and succeeding. Keep moving forward anyway. I've got a flashlight to help light the way.

In this session I'll be right beside you as you come face-to-face with sneaky Ogres getting in the way of your greatness. I'll show you how to release and replace them to so you can live your vivid and extraordinary life.

Let's go get those Ogres!

What's an Ogre?

You are definitely on your way to Vivid Living.

For some of you, doing the exercises and explorations in the previous sessions was just what you needed to jump right into living the vivid and extraordinary life you had always hoped to live. For others, this was just the beginning.

Did you find some roadblocks along your Vivid Living journey? The biggest roadblocks are usually your own internal ones – the naysayers or the voices of fear, doubt, or sabotage that hold you back and keep you from your greatness.

I call these voices Ogres. Releasing their powerful hold can actually be the most challenging and important work of all. Once you loosen their grasp and keep walking toward vivid and extraordinary living, you'll be unstoppable.

So, what exactly is an Ogre, you ask? **An Ogre is any limiting thought, belief, or pattern.** It is a learned or inherited internal response. Ogres are the enemy of change. Their job is to maintain the status quo. Your Ogres want you to feel bad and disempowered. They want you to waste time by reliving the past, worrying about the future, and analyzing everything.

Ogres may sound like the voices of others in your life – voices that at one time may have sounded supportive or helpful. At this point, however, these voices no longer serve you and actually get in the way of vivid and extraordinary living.

Ogres want you to believe that they have your best interest at heart and that their primary purpose is to serve and protect you. In actuality, they are intent on making you miserable. They hold you back from being YOU. They distract you from your truth and all things wise, pristinely pure, deeply happy, and absolutely true at your core.

At one point their messages may have served you. But, at this point, all they do is keep you from living the life you were meant to live – you know, that amazing life full of passion and richness.

Right about now, as you get closer than ever to Vivid Living, your Ogre voices may be getting louder and stronger. If you do in fact start living a vivid and extraordinary life you love, they will become unemployed and homeless. They will no longer have a purpose. So, they'll do anything they can do to keep the status quo.

They are sneaky and slimy and can morph into many different shapes and appearances to try to get you to stay right here where you are. THEY are the ones who are afraid – no, terrified! – of change, not YOU (the true YOU!).

Absolutely everyone has Ogres! Everyone! In most cases, the difference between people who are living vivid lives they love and those who aren't is that the people living vivid lives don't let their Ogres run the show. They have released themselves from the powerful hold of the Ogre. They know how to find, listen to, and trust their truth – not the Ogre.

If you still aren't completely sure of what an Ogre is, here's a list of a few of the most popular Ogres (limiting thoughts, beliefs, or patterns) that I've heard over the years from my clients. You can fill in the blanks below.

1. I'm too old to….

2. I'm too young to….

3. I don't have enough experience to …

4. If I say no then people won't like me.

5. I have to stay in my current job to make a living.

6. I'm too busy to …

7. I'm too tired to …

8. I don't have enough time to …

9. If my mom or dad would have been ….
then I'd be ….

10. When I have/am …, *then* I'll be happy.

11. If he/she would change *then* I'd be happy.

12. It's probably not going to work/happen anyway.

> How do you hold yourself back or stop yourself from Vivid Living? What do you say to yourself and what do you believe about others or the world that holds you back?

Truth or Ogre? Your Body Knows!

How do you tell the difference between an Ogre and your truth? Once again, look to your body. Your body knows!

Let's get to know your truth. Think of a time when you felt really joyful and peaceful, or go back in time to a Peak Experience of yours – a time you felt truly alive, powerful, or unstoppable – the most YOU.

When you remember this time, notice what happens in your body. Maybe you notice a smile spreading across your face, an energy pulsing through your body, a tingling in your arms or legs, a deepening of your breath, a feeling of calm, ease, and flow, or any number of other sensations.

Make note below of whatever it is you notice in your body when you remember this experience. These sensations are a guide to your truth. When you experience these or similar sensations in your body, you know you are thinking or doing something that taps into your truth – into YOU.

_____

_____

_____

_____

_____

Here is a Peak Experience of mine – a time when for a few days I tapped into my absolute truth and was fully ME! One year, as I was transitioning from the world of being a psychotherapist to the world of being a life coach, I attended an Organizational Development (OD) conference in Vancouver, BC. When I arrived, I met a group of young, vibrant OD professionals. I took a risk and shared with them ideas I had about where I was heading, personally and professionally. They were supportive, welcoming, and introduced me to some of their mentors. I was excited, networked a ton, took risks, and felt absolutely unstoppable!

In my body, I noticed unending energy (it was hard to sleep at night I was so excited), lots of smiles from ear-to-ear, and an energized calmness. I loved who I was being and most of the time there was not an Ogre in sight.

This is another great way to know you have tapped into your truth: when there are no Ogres to be found. There is absolutely no room for the Ogres when you honor or live into who you truly are. There's no room for them when you do the things that ground, enliven, or excite you most.

Think about this yourself. Imagine that joyful time or Peak Experience again. Were there any Ogres around? If there were any Ogres hanging around, I imagine they were on the outside looking in and were certainly not running the show.

Another place to find your truth is to look to your Essences and Life Purpose. Your Essences are who you are at your core and your Life Purpose is your Big Intention and the Unique Impact you have on the world around you. When you honor or live into your Essences and Life Purpose you also live into your truth – without your Ogres.

Right now close your eyes, take three breaths, and imagine yourself living into an Essence or your Life Purpose fully. See yourself embodying that Essence or your Life Purpose. Breathe it deeply into your heart and cells. Notice what sensations are present for you in your body. You can be certain that when these same sensations pop up for you at other times, you are aiming right toward your truth. Make note of the sensations here. *If this vision feels scary, hard, or heavy, that's a good sign that the Ogres have hopped on board. Ask them to step aside, or just move them aside yourself and let yourself drink in the vision, Ogre-free.*

_____

_____

_____

_____

_____

_____

Here's a time when I knew I was tapping into my truth. My husband, Ken, and I had been married for a year when we decided to move from Chicago to San Diego. I had lived in Chicago practically my whole life. It was home. Ken and I decided we wanted to try living in another city together before starting a family.

I was scared out of my mind. I was uncertain and anxious as I left behind a lifetime of family and friends – everything that was familiar. At the very same time, when I talked or thought about our move I noticed an aliveness in my body, a smile on my face, a tingling in my arms, and fullness in my heart. I was moving to San Diego from a place of truth and strength. Although my Ogres (fears and anxiety) popped up at times (sometimes a lot!), I didn't let them run the show. It was a great move!

Think of a time when you felt paralyzed, stuck, anxious or frazzled. What sensations do you notice in your body – maybe tightness, heaviness, pain, constricted breathing, deadness, or lack of any flow or energy in your body? When you feel these sensations in your body, then you know an Ogre is leading the way. Capture the sensations here.

_____

_____

_____

_____

_____

_____

> Notice what it is like in your body when you imagine embracing your Life Purpose and Essences fully (without any fears or anxiety and fully surrendering to your amazing vision). *When you fully live into your Life Purpose and Essences, the Ogres are nowhere to be found.*

Debby's Story

Debby, a mom of three, realized Essences taken in the wrong direction can lead her right to her Ogres instead of to her truth.

Family is a very important Essence of Debby's. In fact, when we first started working together, she put family above all else, including above herself (one of the reasons she sought out life coaching). A "Family" Ogre was definitely running the show for her.

When it came to defining her Life Purpose, here is what she created: "I am the glue that holds everyone together and connects us." When she stated her Life Purpose Statement I could hear the tightness and heaviness in her voice and noticed heaviness in my heart. I asked her if she noticed being enlivened or excited when she stated her Life Purpose Statement and she answered with a resounding, "No!"

The Life Purpose Statement she developed was one created by her Ogres and not by her pure truth and Essences. When she focused on the sensations in her body, she knew her Ogres were running the show. She then uncovered a truer statement that is still a work in progress for her but felt much lighter in her body and energized her: "I am the leader who helps people figure things out and gives advice to bring us closer together." This was definitely a lighter and truer statement for Debby.

Truth or Ogre? Other Ways to Know

Besides looking to the sensations in your body to help determine if a thought or belief is an Ogre or not, here are other clues an Ogre is in charge:

- When you think others have to change in order for you to feel better.

- When you hem, haw, and second-guess yourself.

- When your fears are out of control or paralyzing.

- When you hear yourself say or think:

    - "I should, must, ought to…"

    - "I can't…"

    - "I need…"

    - "I don't deserve…"

    - "I have to…"

- When you feel anxious about doing something you know is right for you so you don't do it.

- When you give up, give in, tolerate, or compromise when it doesn't feel right.

> When do you give your power away?

Why are My Ogres Getting Louder?

One of the most important things to remember about Ogres is that as you get closer and closer to Vivid Living, your Ogre voices will get louder. The only job they have ever known is to make you miserable, and they are terrified of being unemployed. They are sneaky, slippery, and change their form and message as they get desperate. Expect them to get loud, obnoxious, or insidious. Note that just because they are loud and repeat themselves does not mean that they are real or true.

In most cases, once you know your Essences, Life Purpose, and can recognize your BodyTruth, what keeps you from Vivid Living is your Ogres.

> What does it look like and feel like to keep moving forward toward vivid and extraordinary living in spite of the fears and doubts that pop up?

Andre's Story

Andre followed his dreams and passions and moved his wife and children to Europe, left his corporate job, and started his own life coaching practice. He was three months into building his practice when I talked with him and heard that his Ogre, which was committed to the status quo of Andre feeling unfulfilled and miserable, was getting sneaky and louder than ever. His Ogre didn't want to let Andre create the kind of success for himself he had always imagined – and Andre sure was getting close!

In addition to working with individual coaching clients, Andre wanted to lead workshops and training for small business owners. He immediately dismissed the idea and explained that he didn't have enough experience so no one would hire him. His sly Ogres were on the loose!

While he's right that he may not have had specific experience leading workshops and training for small business owners, when he pushed his Ogres aside he could sense that he did have much to offer this population. Being a small business owner and living his dreams would make him attractive to many potential clients in his niche.

You can see how he was well on his way toward realizing his dreams. He was experiencing much of the life he had always wanted – living in Europe with his wife and children and starting his coaching practice – when, BAM!, his Ogres popped up and kept him from moving forward. They inhibited him from truly embracing, in every way, a vivid and extraordinary life he loves.

See how sneaky these Ogres can be? They can seem so practical and logical – like they are even there to protect and serve you. Really all they are doing is stealing away your passion and strength, ultimately making you absolutely miserable.

Just because something is uncomfortable, different, difficult, or even scary for you doesn't mean it is a wrong or bad choice. In fact, sometimes when something is uncomfortable or scary, you may still feel curious, energized, excited, or buzzed when you think about it. If this is the case, you can know and trust that you are heading in the right direction – just like Andre.

There's a Monster in the Bathroom

What happens if you are scared of confronting your Ogres? Some of my clients know it would be really helpful to confront them, but the idea of looking these monsters in the face can be terrifying. Does this sound like you? If so, read on.

The other night my 5-year-old daughter was on the way to the bathroom to brush her teeth before bed. It was already dark out. As I finished washing dishes in the kitchen she called to me, "Mom, can you turn on the light in the bathroom?" I was in a cleaning groove, and didn't want to be interrupted. I encouraged her to do it on her own and said jokingly, "There are no monsters in the bathroom." Then she started crying and said, "Yes there are!" I put down the dishes and headed over to give her a hug. I assured her there were no monsters in the bathroom, but, unconvinced, she showed me the light shining through the window that looked like a face.

We walked into the bathroom together, hand-in-hand. My daughter walked slowly, with trepidation, and held my hand tightly. She repeated again that there was a monster in the bathroom. I said, "Let's see," and flipped the light switch. There was not one monster to be found. It was just the light from our neighbor's house shining through our window.

My daughter was definitely relieved. We talked about how next time she got scared of the lights, she could repeat to herself that they are just our neighbor's lights instead of making up the story that there's a monster in the bathroom and scaring herself.

Naming and shining light on your Ogres will feel exciting and liberating for some and may feel terrifying for others. One client talked about how terrified she was and how it was hard for her to focus on doing this important and powerful work. Her Ogres were scaring her silly!

Jeneen's Story

Jeneen is a belly dancer, yoga instructor, and art teacher who is also a mom of two, and lives in Virginia. She shared her fear of diving into this Ogre work with her Vivid Living Coaching Group. "We were moving along so nicely in our group talking about these energizing and exciting things like Essences and Life Purpose then it felt like we were heading into a dark spot, a cave – I didn't want to go there at all. It was scary. I didn't set aside even a minute to spend on the exercises all week.

It took me one-and-a-half weeks, but once I gave myself an hour to start writing about my Ogres it didn't feel anywhere near as scary or hard as I was thinking it would be. I felt much lighter afterward. It is like when I look at them or shine a flashlight on them they shrink immediately. This is really deep, powerful, and important work.

My husband is traveling again and this week I noticed all the Ogre voices that pop up when he's gone and I'm here alone with the kids.

Here's one Ogre Voice: 'You can't do this and handle the kids, your job, and the housework when he's gone!' I tapped into my True Voice instead and now anytime I hear that Ogre voice I breathe and say, 'I can do this!' It is really simple and really basic, but, wow, did it help.

Repeating my True Voice over and over in place of my Ogre voice made me feel like I absolutely COULD do it. I went from feeling like a total wreck to feeling secure and confident. It really shifted EVERYTHING."

Jeneen's experience powerfully illustrates how simply flipping the light switch in the bathroom (even though it may feel scary), can help you uncover the truth – your truth. It is simple to do but not always easy. The Ogres you have running around your life are much scarier in the dark. So flip that light switch, see how powerless and small your Ogres really are, and listen to your truth. Your truth is much more powerful than your Ogres will ever be!

How can facing your Ogres set you free?

Ogre Release and Replace Formula

The Ogre Release and Replace Formula (R & R Formula) below has helped many of my clients (and me) create vivid and extraordinary lives. Freedom, flow, ease, and more R & R (Rest & Relaxation) is all yours on the other side of the Ogres.

Do you think that you have some Ogres running around your life? Want more freedom, ease, and R & R? Then, let's go find these sneaky little things.

Ogre Release and Replace Formula – (R & R Formula)

1. **Name It.**
2. **Release It.**
3. **Replace It.** Find Your True Voice
4. Repeat these steps as often as necessary.

Name it. The first step to take to "get" your Ogres is to notice and name them. If you find you are scared to look your Ogres in the eye or if you think your Ogres have grown, multiplied, or gotten stronger in the dark, then muster all your courage, take that leap of faith, and go find your Ogres anyway. Take a flashlight with you by trusting yourself and the process. When you shine light on them and expose them they will shrink. You'll see how ridiculous they look and how powerless your Ogres really are.

Release it. Once you see them for the meaningless, meek, unattractive, powerless creatures they are, you can banish them or send them away. I've had clients put their Ogres in a box, send them to the moon, run them over with a car, put them out on the ledge of their office building, or send them to an Ogre party. An Ogre party is where all of your Ogres hang out and make each other miserable instead of making you miserable. Notice how freeing it is and how light you can feel when your Ogres are out of the picture.

Replace it. Find your True Voice. Now there is room to tap into and hear your True Voice – the voice from your heart (HeartTruth), core, and spirit that will replace the Ogre voice.

Look to your body to find your True Voice. When you tap into it, you will most likely notice sensations in your body similar to those you experienced when you discovered your Essences and knew you had created your unique Life Purpose Statement. Any time the Ogre voice pops up you can send it off and replace it with your True Voice.

I'm not suggesting that you try to eradicate or fight your Ogres. The minute you engage them in any kind of fight or discussion, they're running the show. Instead, hear them, name them, and then walk right past them toward Vivid Living! The Journal and Action Exercises in this session will empower you to notice and replace your Ogres, not to fight them.

When I started my coaching business, I had lots of Ogres running the show. Here is how I used the Ogre Release and Replace Formula to find my truth.

In my early years as a coach, I had many moments on calls with clients when things would be humming along. We'd be in a groove and I could hear and sense my client's excitement and learning. Upon ending the call, one of my Ogres would pop up and tell me about all the things I did wrong. I'd begin to convince myself I was a horrible coach. My business was growing, but it felt HARD to move forward. I second-guessed myself a lot.

Often, when I hung up the phone, no matter how spectacular the call was my "You Messed Up and Suck" Ogre voice would start chattering away and steal all of the fun and joy out of being in a career that I loved. I felt heavy in my body, lifeless, and stuck.

I decided enough was enough and I was done with the "You Messed Up and Suck" bully running the show. I knew I could never live a life I loved if that Ogre was in the driver's seat.

I knew it was impossible to eradicate the Ogre. And, I knew that the Ogre Release and Replace Formula could help. First, I became vigilant and committed to paying attention to my body, and truth. Next, I released my Ogre by sending it off to play with other Ogres of mine (they got to have a grand time making each other miserable) at an Ogre party.

Then, I slowed down and listened to my True Voice. The true message from my heart was, "You did some great coaching on that call – let's celebrate. Let's also see where there is still room to learn, grow, and become even better." So, I did just that. I celebrated what was great about the coaching call and I owned what I still had to learn and wanted to do differently next time.

I practiced and practiced and celebrated. I learned a lot. I succeeded and failed wildly. I didn't give up. To this day, that Ogre still occasionally pokes its head out. But now I know just what to do to. I come right back to the Ogre Release and Replace Formula and tap into my True Voice. I get right back to vivid and extraordinary living.

> What's possible for you when you replace your Ogre voices with your True Voice?

Get Those Ogres

SESSION HIGHLIGHTS

- Ogres are internal roadblocks to Vivid Living. They are the naysayers: the voices of fear, doubt, or sabotage that you hear in your head. They are any limiting thought, belief, or pattern. Ogres are the enemy of change. They are committed to maintaining the status quo. They hold you back and keep you from your greatness.

- Just because Ogres are loud and repeat themselves often does not mean that they are real or true.

- Everyone has Ogres! In most cases, the difference between people who live vivid and extraordinary lives they love and those who don't is that the people living lives they love don't let their Ogres run the show.

- You know you've found an Ogre when you notice heaviness, darkness, or "stuckness" in your body. Your body knows when an Ogre is running the show!

- When you hear yourself say or think, "I should, must, ought to…I can't…I need…I don't deserve…I have to…," you know an Ogre is running the show.

- **The Ogre Release and Replace Formula** – (R & R Formula)
    1. **Name It.**
    2. **Release It.**
    3. **Replace It.** Find Your True Voice
    4. Repeat these steps as often as necessary.

Finding and naming your Ogres may feel exciting and liberating or may feel downright terrifying. That's OK. Keep moving forward even with the fear. The Ogres running around your life are much scarier in the dark. So flip that light switch, see how weak and small your Ogres really are, and listen to your truth. Your truth is much more powerful than your Ogres will ever be!

Use the Journal and Action Exercises in this session and the Ogre Release and Replace Formula to help you get your Ogres.

Get Those Ogres

JOURNAL EXERCISES

* *Reminder: No need to do all the exercises. Focus on the one/s that excite or interest you the most.*

1. How do I hold myself back?

2. Pick one area of your life that you want to change from the Vivid Living Thermometer or from your Main Aim. List all the Ogre voices, thoughts, beliefs or negative messages that arise when you think about rating that area at a 10. Repeat for all areas of your life you want to shift or transform.

3. What is possible for me when all Ogres in my life are locked in a box or sent to the moon?

4. How do my Ogres get in my way today?

5. How have I overcome an Ogre in the past?

6. What does it cost me when I let my Ogres run the show?

Get Those Ogres

ACTION EXERCISES

* *Reminder: No need to do all the exercises. Focus on the one/s that excite or interest you the most.*

Pick an Ogre or two to focus on. Vigilantly take yourself through **The Ogre Release and Replace Formula - (R & R Formula)** every time it pops up.

Ogre Release and Replace Formula

Each step can be practiced and explored in more depth in the exercises below.

1. **Name It.**
2. **Release It.**
3. **Replace It.** Find Your True Voice
4. Repeat these steps as often as necessary.

1. **Name It**

    Choose one or more of the exercises below to help you name your Ogres.

    a. **Create an Ogre list**. Choose one thing that you are excited or anxious about shifting in your life. What Ogres – limiting thoughts or beliefs – arise when you think about it? Write down the voices or messages you hear. Get them on paper and out of your head.

    b. **Two-hour Ogre hunt**. Take a two-hour block of time. During this time have a sheet of paper close by and write down any and all Ogre messages that you notice.

    c. **Find an Ogre game**. Every day this week keep your Ogre list nearby. See how many new Ogres you can add to the list each day. Make this a game. How many can you find?

d. **The Vivid Living Thermometer & your Ogres.** Pick one area of your life that you want to change from the Vivid Living Thermometer. List all the Ogre voices, thoughts, beliefs or negative messages that arise when you think about rating that area at a 10. Repeat for all areas of your life you want to shift or transform.

e. **Personify your Ogres.** This is a really fun way to name and learn more about your Ogres. Every Ogre of yours has its own personality, look, and feel. Get to know it. Get really familiar with it so you can recognize it and name it with more ease. At the end of this exercise I'll share with you an example of the personification of one of my Ogres.

   •   Name the Ogre. Describe it physically. What does it look like? How does it smell, sound, and taste? What is it wearing?

   •   Draw or paint it.

   •   What is it saying? You may find that one Ogre is responsible for many messages.

   •   What is it great at?

   •   What is it rotten at?

   •   How has it been helpful?

- When is it loud and running the show?
- When is it quiet?
- Where and how do you notice this Ogre in your body?

Let me introduce you to one of my Ogres: The Bully

The Bully is a mean, cute, stylish, teenager with a gang of friends behind her. She keeps telling me, "You're no good, you can't do anything right, and no one will like you." She teases me endlessly.

The Bully is great at making me feel alone, sad, and hopeless. She gets me believing that I messed up horribly and irreparably. She is rotten at helping me see how great I am at having fun and enjoying life. She runs the show and is loud when I make mistakes (big or little), or may have done something that made someone else feel uncomfortable.

She is quiet when I focus my attention on what I did that was good and really drink that in and celebrate. And, when I pay attention to what aligns me with my truth, core, passion, and Essences, then The Bully is nowhere to be found.

2. Release It

Send your Ogre to #$%&.

Anytime you notice an Ogre, find a place to send it – into a box, to the moon, on vacation with other Ogre friends, out the window, etc. Some clients actually create a dedicated Ogre box – decorated or not – and put pieces of paper with Ogre messages written on it or objects that remind them of their Ogres inside it.

a. Where are you sending your Ogres?

b. How do they get there?

3. Replace It. Find Your True Voice

a. **Breathe**. Close your eyes. Breathe.

b. **Say your Ogre message**. When you are ready say the Ogre message to yourself. What are you aware of in your body when you say this message?

c. **Hear your truth**. Ask yourself what you know is true in your heart and core. Play. Try different messages and pick the one that resonates most in your body. Choose the one that feels solid, right, energizing, or exciting.

d. **Write it down**. In the space provided below, on a separate sheet of paper, or on the Notes page at the end of this session, write down your ogre message. Next to each message, write down your True Voice – what you want to say to yourself to replace the Ogre voice. Once you focus on your True Voice, there is no room for the Ogre voice.

Example:

Ogre Voice

True Voice

"*You'll never keep your commitment.*"

"I am trustworthy."

_____   _____
_____   _____
_____   _____
_____   _____

> Visit www.vividliving.net/freebookdownloads to see the **Top 20 Ogre Busters** – messages to stop your Ogres in their tracks. These are the True Voice Statements I hear most often from clients.

4. Release and Replace Visualization

If you're not sure how to do a visualization then see page 21 for Visualization suggestions.

- a. **Breathe**. Close your eyes. Breathe.

- b. **Imagine**. Imagine a situation arising where your Ogre voices prevail.

- c. **Release and Replace**. See yourself releasing and replacing those Ogre voices with your True Voice. See yourself in your mind's eye and feel yourself showing up differently.

- d. **Breathe**. Breathe in this new experience of yourself. Do this while sitting, laying down, or even while exercising.

- e. **Repeat**. Repeat this visualization with any Ogre message you wish to replace.

What's My Homework

GET THOSE OGRES SESSION VI

What actions or reflections are you committed to do, to practice, or to think about? Let these be things that interest, excite or even terrify you. Challenge yourself!

1.

2.

3.

4.

Create structures. Do you think it might be challenging for you to remember to do your homework or keep your commitments? If so, then pick out some structures to put in place to remind you of them. It's easy to get excited about your commitments and intentions. The hard part is keeping them. Structures can help.

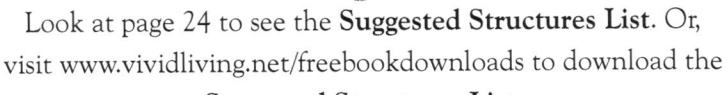

> Look at page 24 to see the **Suggested Structures List**. Or, visit www.vividliving.net/freebookdownloads to download the **Suggested Structures List.**

Vivid Living Resources

SESSION VI

FREE Digital Downloads

⬇ **Top 20 Ogre Busters.** Download a list of 20 powerful Ogre Busters – messages to stop your Ogres in their tracks. These are the True Voice Statements I hear most often from clients.

www.vividliving.net/freebookdownloads

Recommended Reading

Taming Your Gremlin by Rick Carson

Vivid Living Check-In

SESSION VI

1. What have I learned?

2. What challenges did I run into?

3. What do I want to remember that will help me to live a vivid and extraordinary life I love?

4. Fill in a Vivid Living Thermometer today. See what's shifting for you as you journey along your Vivid Living adventure.

VIVID LIVING THERMOMETER   Date _____

AREA OF YOUR LIFE	RATING 0-10
CAREER	
ENVIRONMENT	
FAMILY	
FRIENDS	
FUN	
HEALTH	
ME AS MOM	
MONEY	
PERSONAL GROWTH	
SIGNIFICANT OTHER	
SPIRITUALITY	
OVERALL VIVID LIVING	

AREA OF FOCUS _____
COMMITMENT _____
_____

Build Your Toolbox

SESSION VII

> *Go confidently in the direction of your dreams.*
> *Live the life you have imagined.*
> **Henry David Thoreau**

> *Commitment unlocks the doors of imagination, allows vision,*
> *and gives us the "right stuff" to turn our dreams into reality.*
> **James Womack**

> *The greatest gift you give others is the example*
> *of your own life working.*
> **Sanaya Roman**

You've come so far! You have lots of new tools and much more insight into who YOU really are than you did when you first picked up this book. You have the tools you need to discover what's most important to you, who you are at your core, what your Life Purpose is, and how to use the wisdom of your mind and body to determine what is true for you in any given moment. Fantastic!

Even if you don't feel like every tool has soaked into your cells and life just yet, you still have so much to celebrate! The fact that you made it to this page is HUGE. You carved out time to pick up this book and do something for yourself. No small feat for a busy mom, for sure!

So, celebrate all the tools and nuggets of wisdom you have collected along this extraordinary adventure. Know that there is more – much more to come. It takes time and conscious practice to put these tools in place as a regular part of your life. You are well on your way.

I have a few more thoughts to share during our last session together. During this session, you get to create your very own Toolbox. You get to fill it with the wisdom and tips you want to keep close and remember as you soar into Vivid Living.

It has been an absolute joy and pure pleasure being with you on your journey!

Your Toolbox

Here we are. This is our last session together, for now. Session by session you dove in bravely and boldly. You had this book as your guide, and maybe the support of a buddy, or even a Vivid Living Group.

So, what happens next? You go out and live your vivid and extraordinary life!

But wait!! "Can I do this all alone?" you may ask. Absolutely! You are ready. You have all the tools you need.

You just have to remember to use them. That's why we're going to spend our last session together creating your very own unique Toolbox. You get to take a moment here to capture the juicy tips, tools, and wisdom you've acquired along your Vivid Living journey. Then, you get to put them into your Toolbox. This way you'll have them all at your fingertips, always.

So, what exactly is a Toolbox? A Toolbox is a comprehensive list or actual box full of tips, tools, and structures that you can come back to in the days, weeks, months, and years ahead when things get tough or you want a boost back to vivid and extraordinary living.

You can put anything you want in your Toolbox– anything helpful, inspiring, and fun that reminds you of who you really are and where you are heading.

Once you create your Toolbox, you can reach into it to access tools that will support you to be the extraordinary person you are and to live just the life YOU want to live. The more you practice and use the goodies in your Toolbox, the fewer foggy days you will meet.

Your Toolbox can be a literal or figurative one. I've had clients actually create and decorate a box. Inside they put pictures, quotes, sheets of paper with exercises on them, their coaching journal, songs, and everything that might be a helpful reminder of who they are, where they are going, and how to get there. Or, your Toolbox can simply be a list on a sheet of paper or in a notebook of all the tools, tips, and structures you want to remember. It can even be small enough to put in your purse.

Here's what Jenny has in her Toolbox. She created a box and put all of the items listed below into it. She keeps this box on a table in her hallway and opens it anytime she needs a little pick-me-up or guidance back to Vivid Living. You could even just write these reminders on a piece of paper and hang it up on your fridge, place it on your desk, or put it in your bag.

Jenny's Toolbox

1. This book – **Vivid Living for Busy Moms**
2. My Vivid Living journal
3. A list of the sensations in my body when I'm in a groove
4. The Vivid Living Thermometer
5. My Essence list
6. A reminder to breathe!
7. A reminder to lock my Ogres in a box
8. A list of powerful Ogres and my True Voice

9. A Picture of my Ogres
10. My Life Purpose Statement
11. A reminder to write or journal
12. A reminder to make Body Decisions
13. Four inspiring quotations
14. A reminder to make a Gratitude List
15. A reminder to look at my old Gratitude Lists
16. A list of what all 10's on my Vivid Living Thermometer looks and feels like for me
17. A special rock to remind me of my Nature Essence
18. A photo of when I was little that reminds me of my Freedom and Child-Like Curiosity Essences
19. A photo of my wedding, which reminds me of my Love and Family Essences
20. A photo of my kids playing that reminds me of my Mommy, Love, and Playful Essences
21. An airline ticket from trip to Italy that reminds me of my Adventure, Learning, and Freedom Essences
22. The Celine Dion Song – **That's The Way it Is**
23. A reminder to ask for help when I feel stuck
24. A JumpStart Survey – I can read this for inspiration or fill it out again

> How could creating a Vivid Living Toolbox help you live a vivid and extraordinary life you love?

Nora's Story

Nora, a mom of two little boys, shared that "having a list of the things that I consider part of my coaching Toolbox is great. Everything I want to remember about myself, my life, and what's most important to me is in a little notebook that I can carry in my purse. Sometimes I pull it out when I am stressed or feel like I am going a little crazy. I pull it out and read over my list of tools then and realize that I can help myself. It reminds me that I have so much power inside of me to help myself rather than constantly reaching outside of myself.

The concepts in my Toolbox remind me of concrete ways to tackle any mental conflict I am having. One of the tools in my Toolbox is to write or journal. Writing used to be very difficult for me. When I look at my list of tools and see writing on the list, I am reminded of how helpful it is for me now and how simple it is. It only takes only a few minutes. I've given myself permission to write something short instead of something that is huge or something that I write about and work on for hours and days. My Toolbox has also helped to remind me of the power of visualization and reminds me of my Essences."

Rachel's Story

Rachel is a spunky and insightful client. After doing regular individual coaching together, she knew she was ready to move to an "as needed" basis with coaching – she was ready to be her own life coach. After a few months of coaching herself, here are just a few of the tools she told me she used from her Toolbox regularly.

"First, I have access to new inquiries to help me understand more about what is going on with me and to help me be really present in the moment. Here are some of the inquiries that I come back to often in my Toolbox:

- How can I show up more fully in this situation?

- *What do I know about this (situation, feeling, experience in my body)?*

- *How can I take my 'feeling successful at work' energy and apply it to my personal life so I can feel successful there, too?*

My Essences are another very helpful tool in my Toolbox. Labeling my Essences clearly has given me a sense of entitlement around 'living into' these attributes. When I honor my Essences I honor myself.

And finally, I now have a broad lens of how I view and experience my life. I remember to 'dream big' and 'think big.' My Toolbox is full of invaluable and powerful tools that help me to coach myself."

Just like Jenny, Nora, and Rachel, you can fill your Toolbox with the tools, tips, exercises, visualizations, and reminders that inspire you to be the most amazing YOU possible. Fill your Toolbox with the tools you need to be your own life coach.

> If you were your own life coach, what words of encouragement, acknowledgment and other tools would you give yourself?

The Power of Choice

So, you've got your tools and your Toolbox and you're humming along. Maybe you take your life's temperature regularly using the Vivid Living Thermometer, you listen to your BodyTruth, honor your Essences, and live into your Life Purpose. Maybe your life is feeling full and rich – even booming!

And then you have one of those days. You know one of those days when it doesn't feel quite so easy to honor your Essences, live into your Life Purpose, or to listen to your BodyTruth? Some days you'll easily make choices that are right in line with YOU. And, other days you won't. The difference between the times when you decide to honor an Essence, your Life Purpose, or the wisdom of your body, and the times when you don't, is choice! You now have the freedom of choice.

Once you are aware of your truth, then you get to decide what to do with it. Remember, Vivid Living is not about doing something in your life just because you think you "should" or "have to" – even if it is your truth (that's an Ogre talking). You get to decide how you are going to live your life. You are in the driver's seat, not your Ogres, not anyone else – YOU!

Go ahead and eat that delicious chocolate brownie if you choose to, even if it isn't 100% in line with your Essences. Go ahead and choose to stay in that dead-end job even if you know it takes a toll on your confidence and relationships. Own it, live it, and even enjoy it if you choose it. The power here is that you get to make a choice – in every minute you get to choose. No more living on automatic and letting the Ogres run the show by default.

Abby's Story

Through our coaching work together, Abby, a single mom with two children, understood that her current job was not satisfying or a place she wanted to stay. It actually drained her and took a severe toll on her self-esteem. She didn't like her work, but she did love the hours and flexibility of her job. She was able to pick up her kids from school every day and be with them in the afternoon to do homework and hear all about their day. This was precious time for her.

Even though she knew that her job was toxic for her, she chose to stay in the job for another six months until summer came and her kids' schedules were more flexible and involved less homework. She then began to look for a new job and eventually found one that offered her flexibility and more exciting work.

Before coaching she felt trapped. After becoming clear about her truth and tapping into her Essences, she trusted that she would land on her feet and freely made her choice to stay at her job, for a bit. Our work then focused on how she could keep honoring and living into her Essences and Life Purpose even while working at a job that was far from her ideal vision. You, too, now have full access to the power and freedom of choice.

> What do you choose to say "Yes!" to in order to live a vivid and extraordinary life you love? What do you choose to say "No!" to in order to live a vivid and extraordinary life you love?

Really Foggy Days

What about those days when the skies are gray, and it is foggy and really hard to see beyond the thick, heavy haze that surrounds you? Days may come when it feels like the fog is bigger than just an Ogre or two and all the tools that usually work for you don't work any more. Most of us have days like this every once in awhile.

Sometimes you may actually **choose** to hang out in the fog. Staying there might feel easy, familiar, or exactly like the right place for you to be and explore in that moment. When it is a clear **choice** versus a default pattern, then go for it and really drink it in. At times, I even encourage clients to throw themselves a "pity party." If you are going to choose to hang out there anyway you might as well enjoy it! It can be empowering to **allow** yourself to just hang out in the fog for a bit.

Once you've had enough, however, and you decide you want to get back on the Vivid Living path, you might want a little boost. At times we all need reminders and some extra support to get us back on target. That's when you take out your Toolbox, rummage through it, and reach for those tools that might help move you forward – even an inch. Tool by tool, step by step, your Toolbox can help you manage whatever comes your way as you live a real, perfectly imperfect, vivid, and extraordinary life you love.

> What does it look like and feel like to be present and patient with all of yourself?

Build Your Toolbox

SESSION HIGHLIGHTS

- A Toolbox is a comprehensive list or actual box full of tips, tools, and structures to refer to in the days, weeks, months, and years to come when things get tough or you want a boost back to Vivid Living.

- Know that your Toolbox can be literal or figurative.

- The more you practice and use the goodies in your Toolbox, the fewer foggy days you will meet and the quicker you'll get yourself back to the sunny lands of vivid and extraordinary living.

- In every moment you get to **choose** exactly how you want to live your life. Sometimes you may actually choose to hang out in the fog. Staying there might feel easy, familiar, or exactly like the right place for you to be and explore in that moment. When it is a clear **choice** versus a default pattern, then go for it and really drink it in.

Put on your overalls, reach into the closet, and take down that handy, dandy, tried and true Toolbox. If you look inside of the open box and it's empty, never fear. By doing the Journal and Action Exercises below, your Toolbox will be full and ready to go in no time. Once you fill it up, when you look inside, you'll find many tools to quickly help you get back on your path.

You've come this far. Don't stop now. You've taken the time to do some amazing and inspiring exploration. Take this final step to put it all together for yourself. Use every helpful, delicious morsel this book has to offer. Create your unique, personalized box of tools that will support you to create and sustain vivid and extraordinary living.

Vivid Living for Busy Moms Conclusion

Remember that Vivid Living is not about living a perfect life. There is no such thing. Vivid Living is all about living a vibrant life YOU love. Remember you are human. Keep drinking in and celebrating the highs. Keep feeling the lows. Keep being that fully human, beautiful, inspiring, and amazing YOU that you are.

To quote Marianne Williamson, "As we let our light shine, we unconsciously give others permission to do the same." Go out there and be your best and most amazing self. Live a vivid and extraordinary life you love, and, as you do, you will unconsciously inspire others to do the same.

If I've done my job well, then I've coached myself out of a job. Congratulations! Enjoy living a vivid and extraordinary life you love. Keep believing that Vivid Living is absolutely possible – always. You have all the tools you need. Keep believing in yourself today and going forward! The world is waiting for YOU!

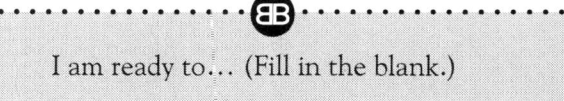

I am ready to… (Fill in the blank.)

Build Your Toolbox

JOURNAL EXERCISES

*   *Reminder: No need to do all the exercises. Focus on the one/s that excite or interest you the most.*

1. **Build Your Toolbox.** What are the tools, inquiries, tips, and statements that stand out from each of the previous sessions that I want to remember? List them below. *Revisit each session's Check-In page.*

    Session I You've Got Yourself a Life Coach
    1.
    2.
    3.

    Session II Take Your Life's Temperature
    1.
    2.
    3.

    Session III Listen to Your BodyTruth
    1.
    2.
    3.

    Session IV Get to Your Core
    1.
    2.
    3.

    Session V Your Life Purpose
    1.
    2.
    3.

>   **Session VI   Get Those Ogres**
>   1.
>   2.
>   3.
>   **Session VII   Build Your Toolbox**
>   1.
>   2.
>   3.

2. When I have been down and out before, what helped me to see the light and get back on track?

3. What do I most want to remember when I feel lost and stuck?

4. Who are the people that I can go to for support when I forget my truth or feel stuck? *You might think of them as your Vivid Living Committee.* What kind of help do I want from each of them? What can I tell them now about how to help me and be with me when I need some extra support later?

5. What are the times when I might need to reach into my Toolbox or reach out for help? *Close your eyes. Breathe and imagine yourself veering off track.* What do I notice in my body? What are the signs/sensations in my body that I need my Toolbox or outside help? What is it like when I finally do reach out for help?

6. What might I be saying to myself when I'm in trouble, get stuck, or hit a road block? *Close your eyes, breathe and listen.*

7. What could get in my way and keep me from living a vivid and extraordinary life I love and what do I want to do about it?

8. What am I going to say "Yes!" and "No!" to in my life to make the changes that I want to make – to live a vivid and extraordinary life I love?

Build Your Toolbox

ACTION EXERCISES

* *Reminder: No need to do all the exercises. Focus on the one/s that excite or interest you the most.*

1. **Do a Vivid Living Thermometer**. See what has changed for you since doing the first Vivid Living Thermometer. What areas are different? What areas are you going to keep focusing on? What are your commitments for each of these areas? You can download a blank Vivid Living Thermometer to fill in at www.vividliving.net/freebookdownloads.

2. **Commit to doing a weekly, monthly, and/or yearly Vivid Living Thermometer**. How often do you want to do a Vivid Living Thermometer check-in? Make a date with yourself to do it. Write it down in your calendar now.

3. **Re-visit and re-score your Main Aim**. This is a great way to see how far you've come on your Vivid Living adventure. Visit your original Main Aim (from your JumpStart Survey, "You've Got Yourself a Life Coach," session I). Then rewrite your Main Aim in the space provided on the next page and score them again today. See how the numbers have shifted from when you first filled out your Main Aim.

4. **Find and decorate a box or container – your Toolbox**. Fill up the box with any/everything that may help to inspire you to live a vivid and extraordinary life you love. Put pieces of paper with the name and/or explanation of any tool, tip, exercise, or structure that

MAIN AIM	SCORE 0-10 10=Most & 0=Least
Example: My life feels balanced. I feel balanced.	3
1.	
2.	
3.	
4.	
5.	

resonated with you into the box. Have the box in plain view. Make it easily accessible.

- a. Organize the tips, tools, exercises, or structures in whatever manner feels exciting or right to you. Anytime you want support or guidance, feel stuck, or want a Vivid Living boost then choose one to three (or more) tools to apply to your life.

- b. Or, put all of the tips,tools, exercises, and structures in a box and when things get rough, close your eyes, reach in and see what you pull out. Apply it to your life.

5. **The Big Step**. This is when you get to take the Big Step (maybe even a big leap) and lock into your cells and body who you are, what you are all about, and where you are heading. This is where you commit to playing big, brave, and bold!

> Visit www.vividliving.net/freebookdownloads to hear me guide you through taking **The Big Step** into Vivid Living.

I'm not taking this lightly. I'm asking you not to either. I'm asking you to make a "no kidding" commitment to yourself! To claim a vivid and extraordinary life you love with all of your heart, mind, body and spirit!

So, let's do it. It's time for you take that step (or leap) into truly living your vivid and extraordinary life!

- a. **Breathe**. Close your eyes and take a few calming and grounding breaths.

b. **Choose your commitments.** What three to five commitments are you making to yourself that will get you closer to vivid and extraordinary living? Close your eyes. Breathe and see what the first three to five items are that come into your mind, heart, or body. Write them down in the blank space below. Make sure that they resonate deeply and feel "right," solid, true, exciting, enlivening, or scary (in a good way).

c. **Make a line.** Find or create an actual line on the ground. You might put a piece of tape on the ground or use a doorway/threshold as a line.

d. **Breathe.** Close your eyes or keep them open. Breathe and really take in who you are today and where you are heading. Imagine it. See it. Feel it.

e. **Commit out loud.** Slowly, say out loud each of the three to five things that you are committing to. Let each word soak into your cells. Imagine everyone you love, everyone who knows and loves you, and vivid and extraordinary living waiting for you on the other side of that line – cheering you on.

f. **Step or leap.** Breathe. When you are ready, hear and see the cheers of encouragement on the other side and feel all the love and support you could ever imagine enveloping you. Take a step (or leap) over the line.

g. **Celebrate**. Look around, take some breaths, and feel yourself in this new place and space. Congratulate yourself. Celebrate. Jump up and down, shout with joy, do a little dance, let those tears flow, or do anything else that feels organic to you in your body and cells.

Congratulations!

Welcome to Vivid and Extraordinary Living!

What's My Homework?

BUILD YOUR TOOLBOX SESSION VII

What actions or reflections are you committed to do, to practice, or to think about? Let these be things that interest, excite or even terrify you. Challenge yourself!

1.

2.

3.

4.

Create structures. Do you think it might be challenging for you to remember to do your homework or keep your commitments? If so, then pick out some structures to put in place to remind you of them. It's easy to get excited about your commitments and intentions. The hard part is keeping them. Structures can help.

> Look at page 24 to see the **Suggested Structures List**. Or, visit www.vividliving.net/freebookdownloads to download the **Suggested Structures List.**

Overall Vivid Living Check-In

Complete this page as you reflect on your overall Vivid Living journey. Then do one more Vivid Living Thermometer. What's changed for you since you did your very first Vivid Living Thermometer?

1. What have I learned?

2. What challenges did I run into?

3. What do I want to remember that will help me to live a vivid and extraordinary life I love?

4. Fill in a Vivid Living Thermometer today. See what's shifting for you as you journey along your Vivid Living adventure.

VIVID LIVING THERMOMETER   Date _____

AREA OF YOUR LIFE	RATING 0-10
CAREER	
ENVIRONMENT	
FAMILY	
FRIENDS	
FUN	
HEALTH	
ME AS MOM	
MONEY	
PERSONAL GROWTH	
SIGNIFICANT OTHER	
SPIRITUALITY	
OVERALL VIVID LIVING	

AREA OF FOCUS _____
COMMITMENT _____

Vivid Living & Life Coaching Resources

FREE Digital Download

⬇ **The Big Step Audio Recording.** Claim your vivid and extraordinary life today!! Download this audio if you want me to guide you to take that Big Step (or leap) into vivid and extraordinary living.

www.vividliving.net/freebookdownloads

Vivid Living Blog

www.vividliving.net/blog

Read my posts and connect with others who are on the path to Vivid Living. Get (maybe even give) some inspiration. We're all in this together!

Life Coaching Websites
Vivid Living and Julie Zeff

www.vividliving.net

Want more vivid and extraordinary living? Contact Julie regarding her availability for individual or group coaching, private workshops, seminars, teleclasses, keynote addresses, or to set up a complimentary coaching consultation.

CTI – Coaches Training Institute

www.thecoaches.com

Train to be a life coach. Over the last 15 years, CTI has trained over 20,000 Co-Active coaches worldwide. Julie trained to be a life coach with CTI.

International Coach Federation

www.coachfederation.org/about-icf
The ICF is one of the leading global organizations dedicated to advancing the coaching profession. The ICF is a wonderful resource if you have any questions about the field of life coaching.

About the Author

Julie Zeff, MSW, CPCC, believes that absolutely everyone can live a vivid and extraordinary life. Her goal is to spread this belief and the tools to actually live it around the globe.

Julie is a life coach and yoga instructor who has worked for over 14 years in the personal growth and mental health fields. She brings the body (and often specifically yoga) into the coaching work that she does and brings life coaching into the yoga that she teaches. Julie teaches her clients to access the wisdom of their body and mind to help them transform their lives.

Her professional mind-body journey began in 1998 when she worked as a Licensed Clinical Social Worker and Massage Therapist. She persistently tried to find a way to combine the two. But, it wasn't until 2002 when she found Life Coaching (CTI, Certified Professional Co-Active Coach - CPCC) and Forrest Yoga (yoga teacher training) that there was a natural and passionate union that transformed her life and career forever.

As a busy, working mom with three children herself, she understands the challenges of trying to find that sweet spot in a busy world of work and family. She uses her own coaching tools each and every day to help her live a vivid and extraordinary life she loves!

Whether through life coaching over the phone, or in a yoga class on a mat, Julie helps her clients tap into the innate truth and wisdom of their body and mind. They learn to make decisions with clarity and confidence. She guides them to courageously shed limiting patterns and beliefs. She helps her clients envision, design, and live their own unique, vivid, and extraordinary life.

Julie was born and raised in a suburb of Chicago and now lives with her husband and three children in sunny Los Angeles, California.

Live a vivid and extraordinary life you love, today!

Want more vivid and extraordinary living? Contact Julie regarding her availability for individual or group coaching, private workshops, seminars, or keynote addresses.

A Complimentary Coaching Consultation for YOU! To find out how Julie can help you live an even more vivid and extraordinary life, contact her to schedule a 30-minute complimentary consultation.

Bring Julie to your next event. Julie is an inspiring, warm, and passionate speaker. Contact her to find out how you can invite her to speak at your next association, club, business, or networking event.

Sign up for the Vivid Living Tidbit. Go to Julie's website to register to receive the FREE monthly e-zine, the Vivid Living Tidbit, full of coaching tips and tools you can use today!

She'd love to hear from you! Do you have a success story to share? Julie would love to hear all about it and possibly feature you in her monthly e-zine – the Vivid Living Tidbit. Email her.

What's Julie Up To? Visit Julie's website to view upcoming dates for Vivid Living Groups, teleclasses, workshops, seminars, and speaking engagements.

Contact Julie Zeff
Website: www.vividliving.net
Email: Julie@vividliving.net

To order additional copies of
Vivid Living for Busy Moms,
visit www.vividliving.net or www.amazon.com
Bulk discounts are available for group purchases.

Made in the USA
Charleston, SC
25 January 2014